CULTURE SMART!
RUSSIA

Anna King

·K·U·P·E·R·A·R·D·

This book is available for special discounts for bulk purchases for sales promotions or premiums. Special editions, including personalized covers, excerpts of existing books, and corporate imprints, can be created in large quantities for special needs.

For more information in the USA write to Special Markets/Premium Sales, 1745 Broadway, MD 6–2, New York, NY 10019, or e-mail specialmarkets@randomhouse.com.

In the United Kingdom contact Kuperard publishers at the address below.

ISBN 978 1 85733 352 7
This book is also available as an e-book: eISBN 978 1 85733 574 3

British Library Cataloguing in Publication Data
A CIP catalogue entry for this book is available from the British Library

First published in Great Britain 2007
by Kuperard, an imprint of Bravo Ltd
59 Hutton Grove, London N12 8DS
Tel: +44 (0) 20 8446 2440   Fax: +44 (0) 20 8446 2441
www.culturesmart.co.uk
Inquiries: sales@kuperard.co.uk

Distributed in the United States and Canada
by Random House Distribution Services
1745 Broadway, New York, NY 10019
Tel: +1 (212) 572-2844   Fax: +1 (212) 572-4961
Inquiries: csorders@randomhouse.com

Series Editor Geoffrey Chesler
Design Bobby Birchall

Printed in Malaysia

Cover image: Catherine Palace, Pushkin, St. Petersburg.
Travel Ink / Philip Craven

About the Author

ANNA KING is a Russian-born business development consultant specializing in cross-cultural issues, negotiation practices, and conflict management. She speaks seven languages, and has an M.Phil. degree from Cambridge University. Anna has worked with key government and decision makers in Britain and across the CIS. She has also interpreted for high-level government visits to the UK and for senior ministerial meetings at the EU in Brussels. Having worked in business development for a number of years for two major British corporations, she is now managing director of the British-based consultancy 3C Negotiations, and is the author of numerous articles and two books on cross-cultural communication.

contents

contents

Map of Russia

introduction

Russia is the largest country in the world, and one of the most enigmatic, complex, and difficult countries to write about. Several stereotypical impressions of Russia are imprinted on our psyche—be it an unsmiling *babushka* in a thin, shabby coat and headscarf or a glamorous model swathed in furs; the echoing crunch of boots on parade in Red Square, or the featherlight grace of ballerinas in Tchaikovsky's *Nutcracker*; the gold Rolex of a nouveau riche, or the shining domes of the Sergiyev Posad Lavra.

Everything in Russia is about contradictions, from its Eurasian geographical position and extremes of climate to its changing economic regimes and conflicting modern values.

Russia's military and political power, as well as the rich contribution of its art and culture, are the result of an inner dynamic not always understood by outsiders. The Russian language and the Russian Orthodox religion are unique; Russian history is tragic; and the people are unpredictable.

It would, of course, be wrong to generalize or to try to pack 141 million people into a single box, extending from Europe to the Pacific. The Muscovite will not behave in the same way as the Kazakh from the southern region of Kuban, the hunter from the far north as the plant worker in the Urals. And yet politicians, writers, and philosophers keep returning to the "enigma of the Russian soul," and referring to the uniquely "Russian way" of behavior and development. Despite the undoubted regional differences there is a shared base of history, tradition, and values.

Travelers to Russia seek answers to the same questions: "What should I expect? How do I make friends? Are there any particular ways of conducting business?" This completely revised edition of *Culture Smart! Russia* sets out to help you become a more perceptive and tolerant traveler, and to make your trip more personally fulfilling. It explores the connections between Russia's turbulent past and its paradoxical present. Using illustrative anecdotes it describes present-day values and attitudes, and offers practical advice on what to expect and how to behave in different social circumstances. It aims to reintroduce the Russian people to you, their generous qualities of character, what they believe, aspire to, and feel, how they entertain, and how they conduct business. If your curiosity extends beyond *matryoshka*, troika, and balalaika, this book is for you. *Dobro pozhalovat!*

culture smart! russia

Key Facts

Official Name	The Russian Federation (*Rossiyskaya Federatsiya*)	Russia is negotiating membership of the World Trade Organization.
Capital City	Moscow	Population 10.4 million
Major Cities	St. Petersburg (second city); population approx. 4 million	Nizhny Novgorod, Samara, Kazan, Perm, Ufa, Rostov-on-Don, Volgograd, and Novosibirsk
Area	6,592,800 sq. miles (17,075,400 sq. km)	The biggest country in the world; about one-ninth of the world's total area
Borders	Norway, Finland, Estonia, Latvia, Belarus, Ukraine, Georgia, Azerbaijan, Kazakhstan, Mongolia, China, and North Korea.	Several former member states of the USSR are no longer contiguous.
Climate	Varies enormously across the huge land area, from the Arctic north to the southerly latitudes of the Black Sea and the moderating maritime influences in the west.	Broadly speaking there is a long cold winter with snow and ice from November to April, a spring thaw from April and May, and a hot summer from June till September.
Time Zones	Russia covers 11 time zones.	Moscow and St. Petersburg are 3 hours ahead of GMT and 8 hours ahead of New York.
Currency	Ruble = 100 kopeks	

Population	Recent estimates give around 142 million, 75% of whom live in cities.	Three quarters of the population live in European Russia.
Ethnic Makeup	81% of the population is Slav, but there are significant minorities.	Minorities incl. Tatars, Ukrainians, Chuvash, Belarussians, Bashkirs, Chechens.
Language	Russian	Other languages also spoken in the autonomous republics.
Religion	Russian Orthodox Christianity	Other religions: Islam, Buddhism, Judaism, and non-Orthodox Christianity
Government	Multiparty democracy with an elected executive president and a bicameral legislature	There are 89 administrative areas, with varying degrees of local autonomy.
Media	The main newspapers are *Komsomolskaya Pravda* and *Kommersant*. The news agencies are Itar-Tass and RIA-Novosti (state-owned) and Interfax (private).	
Media: English Language	*Moscow Times* and *St. Petersburg Times*. Many hotels have internatl. satellite TV.	
Electricity	220 volts, 50 Hz. Two-prong plugs	Adaptors needed for US appliances
Video/TV	PAL/SECAM system	NTSC TV does not work in Russia.
Internet Domain	.ru	
Telephone	The code for Russia is +7. Moscow's code is 495; St. Petersburg's code is 812.	To dial out of Russia, dial 8 (for outside the city), then 10, followed by the country code.

chapter one

LAND & PEOPLE

GEOGRAPHY OF THE SOUL

Contradictions begin from the moment you look at the map. Some American geography books define Russia as "a country in the northern part of Asia." President Putin recently declared that "Russia has extended European borders to the Pacific." Russia has been described as being sandwiched between Asia and Europe, with the Ural Mountains serving as the geographical divide, though "sandwiched" is hardly an appropriate word for a country that stretches from the Baltic Sea to the Pacific Ocean, covers one-sixth of the world's landmass, and extends through eleven time zones.

"We are Scythians! Asians!" wrote the poet Aleksandr Blok in the early twentieth century, yet Russia's contributions to European literature, art, and music are outstanding. While two-thirds of Russia's territory are in Asia, three-quarters of the population live in the European part. Moscow, St. Petersburg, and Yekaterinburg are the largest cities.

Each September the first lesson of the Russian school year traditionally begins with a talk about "our Motherland, and its space one can't embrace." Vast open plains cover most of the territory: the

Eastern European (Russian) Plain, the Mid-Siberian Plateau, and the Central Yakut Plain. It is an eight-hour flight from Moscow to the Pacific coastal city of Vladivostok.

"There is a strong connection between physical geography and the geography of soul, a correlation between the boundlessness of the Russian lands and the Russian spirit. Russian people have in their souls enormous spaces, the boundless eternity of the Russian plains . . . ," wrote the philosopher Nikolai Berdyayev.

"He has a wide soul," Russians often say about somebody sympathetic and supportive.

The enormous Russian spaces have another effect. Visitors cannot but notice that everything is done on a large scale, from architecture to drinking. People you meet, when they open up to you, are larger than life, both in joy and in anger.

In that first lesson of the school year, you would also hear the teacher describe Russia as the richest country in the world, though only the most progressive teacher would add in a whisper, "potentially." Russia has a quarter of the world's mineral resources—from oil, gas, gold, and diamonds to nonferrous metals and timber—but the obstacles of a harsh climate, great distances, and a lack of human resources (Russia has only 2.5 percent of the world's population) have hindered its development. Add to this the permafrost that covers half the landmass, leaving only 8 percent of the land arable; active volcanoes in the Kuril Islands; spring floods and summer forest fires throughout Siberia; and earthquakes on the Kamchatka Peninsula; and you will agree with that progressive teacher.

CLIMATE

Russia encompasses all climate zones except the tropical. Most of the country has a harsh continental climate, with a dramatic difference between summer and winter temperatures. The village of Oymyakon, in the autonomous Sakha Republic, for example, is one of the world's coldest places, with an average winter temperature of -56.6°F (-47°C). A monument there marks the day it fell to -96.16°F (-71.2°C). Global warming might well change things: January 2007 was the first January on record in Moscow without snow.

Southern Russia has a subtropical climate, where year-round temperatures remain above 46°F (approx. 8°C), and summer temperatures range between 79° and 90°F (26° and 32°C), though occasional extreme heat waves might exceed 122°F (50°C).

Winter in Russia lasts much longer than in Europe, and there are only three or four summer months in which concentrated agricultural labor is possible. This may explain the characteristic Russian *shturmovshina*—short bursts of extremely intense work. Short harvest periods and unpredictable weather can lead to risk taking in sowing, and planting *na avos*—a "what if" approach—hoping for a good outcome. And besides, if the harvest fails one can always go fishing. This attitude may go some way to explaining the resilience that is part of the Russian character—the ability to bounce back after losing everything, after forceful relocation due to the whims of politicians, or after economic crises.

RUSSIAN WATERS

Russia's 120,000 rivers stretch for 1,864,114 miles (3 million km); two million fresh and saltwater lakes are scattered across the country. *Volga Matushka*, "Mother Volga," the national symbol of Russia and the longest river in Europe, rises northwest of Moscow and flows all the way to the Caspian Sea. Rivers are extremely important in Russian life; they bring food, transportation, and trade (the famous Nizhny Novgorod trade fair, for example, grew up on the confluence of two major rivers, the Volga and the Oka).

Though Russia is surrounded by seas—the Arctic Ocean, the Black Sea, the Baltic Sea, and the Pacific Ocean—there are huge internal territories that do not have access to seaports. Sociologists talk about the "continental," inward-looking Russian mentality, typical in countries where the majority of the population is isolated from international influences. Most Russian territory is situated more than 250 miles (402 km) from the sea.

THE RUSSIAN FEDERATION

The patchwork of climatic and ecological zones gives rise to different densities of population in the various Russian regions and, inevitably, to ethnic and cultural differences. Geographers have often tried to define those regional parameters. I. Ryazantsev and A. Zavalishin developed the interesting concept of the "Russian cross," which divides the country into four major regions by climatic conditions, culture, and history.

The West: European Russia and the Urals

This area is the cradle of Russian civilization; it has the highest density of population and is the most economically developed. Forty-eight out of fifty-five deposits of natural resources are in the Urals, as well as the major military plants and a huge industrial base. The area was the main laboratory of the Soviet and post-Soviet social and economic experiments, and the main arena of the "battle of minds" between the reformist center and the conservative, provincial "red belt" of Communist supporters.

The East: Southern Siberia, Lake Baikal, and the Southern Part of the Far East

These are the areas around the Trans-Siberian railway and the Pacific coast. The population is less dense here, and there is a strong sense of regional identity. Those who live in Siberia are known as *sibiryaky*, and those who live in the Far East as *dalnevostochniki*.

The *sibiryaky* are tough and hardworking, with a strong survival instinct. They are either the descendants of the Siberian pioneers of the eighteenth century or the grandchildren or children of ex-prisoners: it was in Siberia that the majority of Stalin's camps were situated, and one-third of those who survived their ordeal decided not to return (or were not allowed to return) to Central Russia. The social system of mutual support and camaraderie is stronger here than in other regions.

The *dalnevostochniki*, who live on the Pacific coast, are more detached and self-contained. They are an eight-hour flight away from the central government decision makers. Those who moved here were ready for start-up difficulties, and relied on their own resources and skills.

The Eurasian North
This includes the territories north of around 60° latitude. Here normal agriculture is practically impossible due to the harsh winters, permafrost, and long polar nights. The population consists

mainly of hunters, fishermen, deer herders, and those working in the mining industries.

The South
This includes the autonomous republics of the Northern Caucasus and the basin of the Don

River. The local conflicts here go back more than a century. The Russian Empire gained political control of the Caucasus in the 1860s, and the region, especially the Checheno-Ingush region, has been a constant source of conflict ever since.

The southern mentality represents a melting pot of 112 ethnic groups, mixing the customs of the Kazakhs, whose ancestors escaped from Ukraine in search of freedom, with the aspirations of the local ethnic minorities to preserve Caucasian customs, identity, and independence.

According to the 2002 census, the ethnic groups in the Russian Federation are: Russian, 79.8 percent; Tatar, 3.8 percent; Ukrainian, 2 percent; Bashkir, 1.2 percent; Chuvash, 1.1 percent; others, 12.1 percent.

The Federal Structure

The Russian Federation is divided into eighty-seven administrative units officially known as "Federal Subjects." Of these, thirty are defined by ethnicity, and fifty-seven by territory. According to the constitution all the regional units are equal in their relationship to the center; in reality, there are subtle differences in the degrees of autonomy they enjoy. They are divided into the following categories: twenty-one republics; nine territories (*krai*); forty-eight regions (*oblast*), and nine autonomous regions (*avtonomnaya oblast*, or *avtonomny okrug*). Moscow and St. Petersburg are regional units in their own right and are called "Federal Cities." If you find this confusing, imagine trying to manage and coordinate this entity in a unified way.

Since 2000, President Putin has overseen a sustained recentralization of power in the relations between the center and the "subjects of federation." Russia has been divided into seven federal districts, overseen by presidential envoys (*polpredi*). Five out of those seven envoys are former officers of the security services. Their first task has been to harmonize federal and regional legislation, which in some cases had diverged widely in the 1990s. Budgetary relations between the center and the regions have shifted in favor of the federal government. In December 2004 the President abolished the direct election of regional leaders and reverted to the earlier system, whereby leaders are appointed by the President, subject to approval by the regional legislature. A process has begun of consolidating regions into larger, supposedly more manageable units. The first to merge were Perm Oblast and Komi-Permyak Autonomous Okrug. Further mergers are in the pipeline. But despite those efforts, the relations between the federal center and the regions still follow the *matryoshka*, or Russian doll, principle: "subjects of federation" are self-governing islands of various sizes within one big doll.

GOVERNMENT AND POLITICS

Political analysts both in Russia and abroad have been struggling to find an accurate definition of the present state of the Russian political system. "Sovereign democracy" and "democratic autocracy" are just two attempts. The bottom line, however, remains the same: the Russian president has an enormous amount of power.

The President

The presidency is Russia's key political institution. The president is head of state and commander-in-chief of the armed forces. He has extensive powers to determine domestic and foreign policy. He submits draft legislation to parliament, and signs into law or vetoes the bills that parliament has adopted. He may also issue decrees and directives that have the force of law but do not require parliamentary approval. He is elected to a four-year term by universal suffrage. No individual may serve more than two consecutive terms. In theory at least, this does not rule out the possibility that a president who has served two terms might cede power to a successor and later return to power for a third term. It does, however, mean that, in the current state of affairs, unless the constitution is amended, which Putin has said he does not intend to do, he will be obliged to leave office in early 2008. The constitution makes no provision for a vice president, and there is no specific procedure for determining whether or not the president is capable of carrying out his duties.

As commander-in-chief of the armed forces, the president approves the defense doctrine, appoints and removes the high command of the armed forces, and confers high military ranks and awards. He can declare war, martial law, or a state of emergency on his own initiative and authority, but must obtain authorization from the Federation Council before ordering deployment of the armed forces outside Russian territory.

The Presidential Administration

The president relies for support on the Presidential Administration (PA), which has a staff of two thousand. In theory, the PA confines itself to setting overall policy, while the government implements policy on a day-to-day basis. In practice, this division of labor is blurred, and the PA often intervenes in specific issues. Under Putin's leadership, it has become the norm for federal legislation to be drafted by the PA.

According to Olga Kryshtanovskaya and Stephen White, who have researched the power struggles within the Kremlin, Putin's administration is believed to be divided into several "clans," all of which support a strong or even authoritarian state. On the one hand are the *siloviki*, representing mainly the law enforcement agencies, who favor strong state control of both economy and society but who are believed to be divided among themselves and jostling for power. On the other hand are the so-called liberals, who support a market economy and what they regard as a democratic path of development for Russia. While the *siloviki* support a strong state as a matter of course, even the liberals argue that

Russia's population is not ready for democratic reforms and that the state accordingly has no alternative but to control events from the top.

Parliament

The bicameral Federal Assembly (*Federalnoje Sobranije*) consists of the upper house—the Federation Council (*Sovet Federatsii*) with 174 seats, composed of members appointed from 87 regional "subjects of federation"—and the lower house—the State Duma *(Gosudarstvennaja Duma)*, which consists of 450 elected deputies. Until recently half the members were elected by proportional representation from party lists winning at least 5 percent of the vote, and half from single-member constituencies. The system changed in 2007 to party lists only. In order to qualify for seats, a party has to win at least 7 percent of the national vote.

In Russia executive and legislative power are totally separate; that is, members of parliament cannot become ministers.

Government

In 2004, the number of government ministries was cut from twenty-three to fourteen. The powers of the remaining ministries were extended to include the power to set policy and draft legislation, and they were made responsible for overseeing a number of subordinate agencies and federal services. The government is headed by the prime minister.

In a gesture toward democracy, the president has set up two other bodies: the State Council, representing the governors of the regions and the presidents of the republics; and the Public Chamber, which consists of Kremlin nominees, representatives of NGOs, and prominent public figures. However, the impact of the State Council on policy making has been small, and the role of the Public Chamber is purely consultative.

A BRIEF HISTORY

Recently a French publisher referred to Russia as "a civilization of tears." Russia's history is also one of spiritual strength, defiance against invaders, opposition to reforms from the top, and the ability to survive, live, and love, even through the hardest, darkest times of the police state.

Certain names and events from Russian history —Ivan the Terrible, Peter the Great, Catherine the Great, Rasputin, Lenin, Trotsky, Stalin, the October Revolution, the Battle of Stalingrad, the Cold War, *perestroika*—are familiar to us, even if we don't know much about them. This is a brief introduction to the major events that have influenced and shaped the Russian psyche.

Kievan Rus

The Russians trace their ancestry to the Eastern Slavic tribes. According to legend, three brothers—Kiy, Shchek, and Khoryv, from the Slavic tribe of Polians—founded the settlement of

Kiev in the sixth century CE. They built a town and called it Kyiv, after the eldest brother. In 882 the Scandinavian prince Oleg captured the town, killed the local Polian rulers Ascold and Dir, and proclaimed, "Here will be the mother of Rus cities." (Rus was the dominant Viking clan.) Kiev became an important point on the Viking trade route, called "From Varangians to Greeks," as it extended from the Baltic to the Mediterranean.

In the tenth century Kiev was the capital of the Kievan Rus, a powerful empire that extended from the Baltic Sea in the north to the Black Sea in the south. In 988 Prince Vladimir introduced Orthodox Christianity to Rus, albeit in a peculiar

way. He announced his decision to be christened to the Byzantine Emperors Constantine and Basil, and took his fleet to Crimea, to the Byzantine city of Khersones, for the purpose. Then he returned to Kiev and ordered the pagan wooden idols to be cast down. His subjects watched in horror as the idols floated down the Dnieper River. Vladimir appeared on the hill with the council of Greek priests. At his signal, all the people there, adults and children, stepped into the freezing waters of the river to be baptized.

Kievan Rus flourished during the rule of Grand Prince Yaroslav (1019–54), son of Vladimir the Great. Known as Yaroslav the Wise, he was indeed one of the wisest statesmen of his time. He created the first legal code, called "the Russian truth," carried out grand construction projects, and avoided wars by marrying his daughters to European monarchs. His eldest daughter, Anna, became the first literate queen of France, and signed decrees and letters for her husband.

The prosperity of Kievan Rus attracted invaders from the southern steppes. The city was destroyed by the Mongol chief Baty Khan in 1240. The siege of Kiev lasted several weeks. The Mongol army was so enormous that, according to the chronicler, "You could not hear anything for the creak of their carts, the roar of their camels . . . The land of Rus was filled with the enemy." The city was burned down, and thousands were killed. In the thirteenth century the lands of Kievan Rus became the principalities of Galicia, Volynia, and Muscovy—later Poland, Lithuania, and Russia.

The Tatar Invasion
The centuries-long Tatar invasion locked Russia away from Europe. Led by the mighty Mongol chief Genghis Khan ("Great leader"), the Tatars moved quickly through the steppes and plains and established khanates throughout southern Russia, exacting tribute (*dan*) from each principality. Three hundred years of Tatar reign (*igo*, as the Russians

call it) left traces in the structure of the Russian language, music, and mentality. "With the Russian, scratch the surface—find a Tatar" is a popular Russian saying.

The Rise of Moscow

The emergence of Moscow as the leading Russian city-state began with the victory of Prince Dimitry of Muscovy (later known as Dimitry Donskoy) over the Tatars at the battle of Kulikovo on the Don River in 1380. This victory established the beginnings of Russian independence from the Tatars, though the yoke was not thrown off until the end of the fifteenth century by Ivan III (1462–1505), known as Ivan the Great. The first Russian prince to call himself a Tsar (from the Roman *Caesar*), he conquered Novgorod and turned the Orthodox Church into an instrument of state. By 1505, with a population of 100,000, Moscow was one of the biggest cities in the world.

Ivan the Terrible

It seems that destiny laid a curse on the Russian nation. Its history has been shaped by a number of unstable, impulsive, volatile tyrants who based their reigns on fear. The first in this bloody list was Ivan IV, "the Terrible." The English epithet does not convey the full weight of the Russian name, *Grozny*, which means "causing fear," "threatening," or "formidable." It fully describes the violent, unpredictable character of this tsar, and his ways of dealing with the *boyars*, the Russian nobility. True to his suspicious nature, he would invite them to his palace for overnight feasts and give them only his famous honey brew without food; he hoped that the hungry *boyars* would get drunk faster and reveal their hidden plans and intentions. He was the first to become "Tsar of all the Russians," and established the autocratic rule that lasted until the twentieth century.

The Romanov Dynasty

After a period of civil war and invasions by Sweden and Poland, stability returned to Russia in 1613 with the accession to the throne of Mikhail Romanov. The Romanov dynasty continued to rule Russia until the Revolution in 1917.

The three hundred years of the Romanov dynasty were approximately the years when Russia was looking inward, with its own form of Christianity, its own alphabet, and even its own form of slavery: serfdom replaced the Tatar tributes and remained a sad Russian reality until its abolition in 1861. Years later, Anton Chekhov admitted that he was still squeezing the slave mentality out of himself, drop by drop.

There was one Romanov Tsar who not only looked toward Europe himself, but who dragged Russia there with all his might and his ferocious temper, looming over his subjects from his immense height.

Peter the Great (1689–1725)

"Peter [the Great] accelerated the Westernization of barbaric Russia, not neglecting to use barbarian methods to fight its barbarity . . ." said Lenin of his reforms.

When, after his fact-finding, shipbuilding, carpentry, and statehood-learning Grand Tour of Europe, Peter the Great decided to modernize Russia, he started with the most important concepts and institutions of Russian life: the calendar, clothing, beards, the army, and class privileges. He even established a "merriment police" to spy on people and ensure they were not complaining. Altogether, he introduced more than a hundred reforms and regulations.

His name is immortalized by the city he started building on the bones and blood of thousands of peasants at the mouth of the Neva River in 1703. The "window to Europe," "the Baltic beauty," and "the Venice of the North," St. Petersburg is a city of elegant bridges and Italianate architecture.

Catherine the Great (1762–96)

The imposition of "Europeanness from the top" continued later with the reign of Catherine the Great, who made the Russian capital the center of sophistication, indulgence, art, and literature. Catherine expanded the Russian empire to the west and to the south, and increased Russia's influence in Europe. The scope of her interests was enormous: legislation and medicine, education and architecture. Her decrees established academic centers and libraries not just in the capital, but across the whole empire.

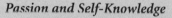

Passion and Self-Knowledge

Catherine once jokingly asked three ambassadors, who were accompanying her on a journey across the Empire, "If I hadn't been an Empress, what do you think my fate would have been?"

"You would have become a wise legislator—but you are one already," was the first answer.

"You would have become a great ambassador," was the next suggestion.

"Or, if you had been a man, you would have been a famous commander," came the third reply.

Catherine laughed. "Oh, my passionate nature would not have allowed me to do that! I would have risked anything for glory, and would have died in the first battle."

Napoleon's Invasion of Russia

The French emperor thought he had conquered Russia when he entered Moscow unopposed in September 1812 with his Grand Army of nearly seven hundred thousand soldiers—the largest European army there had ever been. He did not realize that he had fallen victim to Marshal Kutuzov's cunning plan of strategic retreat. The French found Moscow without Muscovites or food supplies. Their lines were overstretched and their troops exhausted. When the city was destroyed by fire, and with winter approaching, they began their five-hundred-mile march home. Kutuzov blocked retreat by a milder southern route, and forced the French to retrace their steps through the devastated countryside. What had been planned as a victorious summer campaign ended as a rout on the frozen fields of Russia. Around thirty thousand men were all that remained of this vast army. After this decisive victory there was a universal stirring in Europe against the French. Tsar Alexander I himself led Russia's armies into Germany in 1813, where they took part in the battles of Dresden and Leipzig. In 1814 the Russian army entered Paris with the other victorious Allies.

There are stories about Russian Cossacks marching through Europe shouting "*Bystro!*" ("quickly!") when they wanted a snack in a tavern, and allegedly thus giving the name to modern French bistros. For the young Russian officers commanding the troops this was an opportunity to experience life in countries without serfdom and autocracy. They brought new, democratic ideas home with them, and a growing dissatisfaction with the tsarist regime.

The Decembrists

In December 1825 a group of idealistic Russian officers attempted to overthrow Tsar Nicholas I in order to bring about the adoption of a constitutional monarchy. This was the first uprising of the ruling classes, as opposed to a peasant mutiny. The rebellion was doomed: the Decembrists were defeated by loyal troops and executed or exiled to Siberia. Nicholas I famously commented, "I hate those who oppose me and despise those who serve me . . ."

The Abolition of Serfdom (1861)

In response to the growing demand for reform by the Russian intelligentsia, serfdom was abolished under Alexanders II and III. Peasants began leaving the land to work in the cities, factories, and on the railways, and industrial life developed.

Agriculture, however, remained backward. The abolition of serfdom encouraged liberal reformers and socialist revolutionaries alike. During this period Central Asia and the Far Eastern port of

Vladivostok came under Russian control, and Russia sold Alaska (settled as a trading post in 1784) to the United States for 7.2 million dollars.

THE TRAGIC TWENTIETH CENTURY

The twentieth century is the darkest page in the Russian history of tears and a huge subject in its own right. Two world wars, the Revolution of 1905, and the Great October Socialist Revolution of 1917, the civil war between the Reds (the Bolshevik forces) and the Whites; the establishment of CheKa-NKVD-KGB, the rise of Stalin and his reign of terror, turning the whole country into a Gulag: there are millions and millions of lost lives behind the dry lines of the following paragraphs. If you wonder why Russians don't smile in the streets, remember these pages.

The 1905 Revolution

At first the government's policies to develop industry were successful. Then a series of poor harvests, an industrial slump, and hardship caused by a disastrous war with Japan brought social tensions to the boiling point. On January 22, 1905, a peaceful crowd of 200,000 people marched to the Winter Palace in St. Petersburg to deliver a petition to Tsar Nicholas II demanding better working conditions. They were cut down by his Cossack troops.

This massacre, known as "Bloody Sunday," was the last straw. Within a week there were outbreaks of strikes all over the country, including mutinies in the navy. Activists in Moscow and St. Petersburg set up worker's councils, called Soviets, with representatives chosen by popular acclaim. These became the foundation of the new revolutionary system of government after 1917.

In 1906 the Tsar gave way to the demand for representation by permitting an elected parliament, or Duma. Prime Minister Pyotr Stolypin introduced reforms that allowed peasants to buy large parcels of land. This led to the creation of a class of prosperous peasant farmers, the *Kulaks*.

The 1917 Revolution

When the First World War broke out in 1914, Russia joined Britain and France against Germany and the Austro-Hungarian Empire. A series of heavy defeats exposed the ineffectiveness of the government. The war caused poverty and hunger, and support for the Tsar drained away. Two alternative power groups developed: the Duma, periodically disbanded by the Tsar, which attracted the educated and commercial classes, and which formed a Provisional Government; and the Soviets, which attracted soldiers and factory workers, that now sprang up all over the country. At first the two cooperated, demanding the abdication of the Tsar. Nicholas abdicated on March 15, 1917, in the face of the German threat of invasion and a revolt by his own troops.

The Provisional Government, led by Alexander Kerensky, decided to continue the war, which was a huge mistake. This unpopular policy was

opposed by Lenin (Vladimir Ilyich Ulyanov), leader of the Bolshevik wing of the Marxist Social Democratic Party, under the slogan "Bread, Peace, Land." On November 6 and 7, 1917, the Bolsheviks seized power in Petrograd (as St. Petersburg had been renamed), and arrested the entire government. Kerensky escaped to exile, and Lenin became head of government.

In December 1917 the new Bolshevik government signed an armistice with Germany, set up a secret police force (the CheKa, forerunner of the NKVD and the KGB), and founded the Red Army. The Bolshevik Party renamed itself the Communist Party and moved the capital from St. Petersburg to Moscow.

The Communists were opposed by an alliance of anti-Bolshevik forces supported by Britain, France, Japan, and the USA. Under Leon Trotsky (Lev Bronstein), the Red Army became a formidable fighting machine. Fearing that the Tsar might become a rallying point, the Bolsheviks murdered the royal family at Yekaterinburg in the Urals in July 1918. The bitter civil war finally ended in 1921 with a Communist victory. In 1922 the Union of Soviet Socialist Republics was formed, with Lenin as its head—a multinational, socialist empire based on the borders of Imperial Russia.

Joseph Stalin (1879–1953)

On Lenin's death in 1924, Joseph Stalin (Iosif Dzhugashvili) outmaneuvered his charismatic rival Trotsky and became General Secretary of the Communist Party. He set out to transform Russia into a powerful modern industrial nation through centralized state planning. To feed the growing numbers of workers, he forced the peasants into collective farms *(kolkhoz),* and instituted three Five Year Plans, with the result that by 1939 the USSR was an industrial world leader. To enforce his goals, Stalin created a totalitarian state, purging the Party and the country of all who might oppose him. He used the NKVD to keep the population terrorized and extended the practice of exiling dissidents to labor camps by setting up the *gulags,* an acronym of *Glavnoe Upravlenie Lagerey (*Main Administration for Camps). By 1939 over twenty million Russians had  been transported to labor camps, of whom about twelve million died. The last camp inmates were released only in 1992, by Boris Yeltsin.

The Great Patriotic War

Stalin signed a nonaggression pact with Hitler in 1939 that secretly ceded eastern Poland to Russia and gave Russia a free hand in the Baltic. Despite this, in June 1941 Hitler's armies invaded Russia, only grinding to a halt at Stalingrad on the Volga in 1942, in one of the most savagely fought battles of the war. Like the French in 1812, the Germans were forced to retreat during the freezing Russian winter, the Red Army following them all the way and finally entering Berlin in 1945. Enormous sacrifices were made by Russia during the Second World War—at least twenty-six million died, including a million at Stalingrad.

The Cold War

After the war, the Soviet Union controlled most of Eastern and Central Europe through puppet Communist regimes answerable to Moscow. To rival NATO, in  1955 the satellite Communist states were locked into a military alliance with the Soviet Union called the Warsaw Pact. The state of tension between the Soviet Union and the Western powers led by the USA became known as the Cold War—an ideological and military war with limited armed conflict, but overshadowed by the threat of nuclear weapons.

Glasnost and *Perestroika*

Following Stalin's death in 1953 a collective leadership assumed power in Russia. Nikita Khrushchev introduced a policy of liberalization and denounced the errors and crimes of the Stalin era at the 1956 Party Congress. Despite a conservative backlash in the Party, ordinary people became increasingly aware of the scale of the failures and anomalies of the Communist system, and in 1986 the relatively young General Secretary, Mikhail Gorbachev, introduced reforms promoting *glasnost* (openness) and *perestroika* (restructuring). He also moved to reduce the huge stockpile of nuclear weapons held by the USA and the USSR, and to withdraw troops from abroad.

The policy of *glasnost* fanned nationalist demands for independence among the Soviet republics of the Baltic and Transcaucasia. Gorbachev responded to these by declaring "the Sinatra doctrine"—letting them do it their way, after the Frank Sinatra song "My Way."

In foreign policy, the Cold War was formally ended at the Malta summit between Gorbachev and President Bush in 1989, opening up the possibility of GATT membership and Western investment. This move was rapidly followed by the reunification of East and West Germany in 1990. Meanwhile the republics of the USSR were beginning to seize on changes being made in the constitution to flex their muscles.

The "reform-communist" Boris Yeltsin took power as President in the Russian Federation, while many of the conquered states began to push for unilateral independence. In 1991 five republics—the Russian Federation, Kazakhstan, Belorussia, Tajikistan, and Uzbekistan—signed a new, more truly federal Union Treaty, replacing the 1922 USSR treaty. It was accepted that Estonia, Latvia, Lithuania, Georgia, Armenia, and Moldova would not sign.

The Abortive Anti-Gorbachev Coup
In 1991 an attempted *coup d'état* by the Communist Party old guard, the KGB, and the military was faced down in Moscow by Boris Yeltsin. He resisted them as head of a democratic "opposition state" based at the Duma building, known as "the White House," just over a mile from the Kremlin.

Unable to capture the White House, or win public approval or international recognition, the coup collapsed. Over the next six months Yeltsin became the engine of radical democratic change. The old Communist structures began to crumble and a new dawn of grassroots capitalism emerged, from trading in Ismailovsky Park to setting up restaurants and canteens in student basements.

The failed coup hastened the disintegration of the USSR, and some of its constituent republics became independent states (Estonia, Lithuania, Latvia, Ukraine, Moldova, Georgia, and Kazakhstan). The Soviet Union was formally dissolved on December 25,1991, when Gorbachev resigned as president, and eleven of the former Soviet republics came together in the Confederation of Independent States (CIS), with Yeltsin as president and prime minister.

In Russia the Communist red flag with its hammer and sickle was replaced by the traditional Russian red, white, and blue tricolor. Russia was now a Federation, and a member of a loose confederation of some of the former republics of the Soviet Union. The new Russian constitution was formally promulgated in 1993.

Up to Date

"It is much easier to break than to build," is a well-known Russian proverb. The introduction of *perestroika* illustrates the point. The old Soviet system was demolished, but building a new one turned out to be a much harder task. In 1992 and 1993 the sudden abolition of price controls led to hyperinflation, wiping out all savings. In 1992 alone prices increased twenty-six times. In 1998 people's savings, and the emerging middle classes, were wiped out again with the ruble crash.

Disillusionment with the present led many to romanticize the past—both regretting the loss of the old "law and order," and taking a nostalgic interest in all pre-Soviet Russian history. There is a continuing debate and reevaluation of various historic events in the press and in everyday conversation. If you are prepared to discuss history, tread carefully. It is a sensitive subject, and you might offend somebody without realizing it.

RUSSIAN SOCIETY TODAY
Demographic Trends

Data published by Goskomstat, the Russian Committee on Statistics, shows some disturbing demographic trends. In 2005 the population of Russia was 144.7 million. In 2013, according to the demographers, it will be 133 million. In the last thirteen years deaths exceeded births by 11 million. In the year 2000 life expectancy was 73 years for a woman and 58.9 years for a man. To counter this trend the President announced a new demographic program, "Give birth to a Patriot," which offers financial benefits to mothers with two or more children.

Five million people, according to Goskomstat, moved above the poverty level in the last five years; this leaves 25 million people still below it.

Social Classes
The Elite

The prominent sociologist Tatyana Zaslavskaya describes the Russian elite as "a stratum of individuals and groups that have official or unofficial authority to make decisions at state level." These several tens of thousands of politicians, top businessmen, and senior civil servants are the most powerful group in Russian society. The interests of big business and the state intertwine in a way not seen in the West. Loyalty to those in power is traded for favoritism and "special rules" for the leading corporations. Recent scandals demonstrate the repercussions for those who try to break this mold.

The "New Russians"

The "New Russians" are the main backers of the elite, and their support is rewarded: 15 percent of the population owns 57 percent of the national wealth, while 5 percent are classified as "wealthy." However, this wealth is often relative to Russian, not Western, standards. Only 52 percent of this group own a car; only 40 percent own computers. This is the class that has benefited from the recent market reforms. They are interested in strengthening their position and protecting their property, but have to face covert (and sometimes quite open) hostility from the majority of the population: the gap between the rich and the poor grows bigger every day. You have only to observe the number of Bentleys and Maybachs stuck in Moscow traffic jams, and then venture down into the underground passageways, to witness this stark reality.

The Middle Class

The Russian middle classes are the middle managers, officers, small businessmen, qualified specialists, and heads of department who have been able to adapt to the economic changes. Their problems are the cost and quality of services, health care, and accommodation, but not the cost of milk or bread. The newly born Russian middle class was wiped out by the financial crisis of 1998, and emerged again to constitute, according to various estimates, 15 to 20 percent of the population (in the developed countries it is 70 percent). Sociologists fear that if property prices continue to rise and the quality of health care continues to deteriorate, this class will "vote with their feet" and will make sure that at least their children have a safer, more stable life abroad. Alternatively, they will join the ranks of the 70 percent of the population who live between middle-class standards and poverty.

The Majority of the Russian Population

The bedrock of Russian society includes intellectuals, blue-collar workers, technical staff, and those working in services and agriculture. This is the social group that politicians try to influence, and the development of this class will determine Russia's sociopolitical future.

According to Tatyana Maleva, the director of the Russian Independent Institute of Social Policy, "If this group develops successfully, and thirty-five percent of this group join the middle class, it will tip the balance in the country. However, if these thirty-five percent slide into poverty [where

most retirees, disabled, and migrants already are],
it will lead to a social catastrophe."

The Generations

Twentieth-century society in Russia underwent so
many social transformations, with norms set and
broken so many times, that nowhere else in the
world does every new generation differ more
from the previous one.

Retirees

Now in their seventies and eighties, this is the war
generation. They remember the hardships of
1941–45 well enough still to live by the motto,
"We'll survive anything as long as there is no war."
They are nostalgic about Soviet times, guaranteed
health care, and guaranteed waiting in line, and
are traditionally the most politically active part of
the population. No surprise, then, that the
Pensioners' party was strong and growing fast
before merging with the Party of Justice.

The 1960s Youth

Now aged fifty to seventy, they have seen it all
before: Stalin's fear and denunciation, the thaw of
the 1960s, when they were lulled into the false
hope of "freedom of thought" by Khrushchev—
new poems, new art, new ways of thinking—only
to be pushed into the stagnation of the 1970s, and
to become cynical and bitter. If they were allowed
to think, they were not allowed to voice their

ideas. Their hopes were crushed, and they either live for their children or try to adjust, again.

"Brains and Guts"

Aged thirty-five to fifty, this is the generation of the market reforms. After the collapse of the centralized economy, when the opportunities were all there, they were the ones who created the market—if they had brains, guts, and enough resilience to pay off the bureaucrats and the mafia. Brought up by their 1960s parents, they were taught to be skeptical about the changes and expect the worst. This survival tactic has certainly helped them to succeed in today's Russia.

The Lost Generation

Educated in 1991–95, the last generation brought up to believe in Communism has ended up with a vacuum of faith. Their higher education began when the old textbooks and educational system were being withdrawn, and the new not yet approved. This generation has found it hardest to adjust; it has the highest number of drug addicts, alcoholics, criminals, and unemployed.

The Future of Russia

Those in their twenties and thirties are the first generation to grow up completely without Soviet ideology. This does not mean to say they are not absorbing other ideologies eagerly. This generation has both the largest number of skinheads and neo-nationalists, and pragmatic, goal-driven, highly educated workers. This generation is free not only of the Soviet legacy, but also of the memories of Soviet autocracy, war, and the adjustment to transition.

The sociologist Yury Levada warned about the "problem of memory loss" of the youngest Russian generation: " . . . the political and economic walls of their house were already built for them. The Soviet past is an insignificant part of their lives, if it exists at all. It is the first pragmatic Russian generation in a hundred years that does not possess a historical and social memory of the country's events." This is the generation that will build Russia's future. Do they know what sort of Russia is it going to be?

chapter two

VALUES & ATTITUDES

"National character is nothing but a myth", said the poet Gumilev at the beginning of the twentieth century. And yet there have been many attempts to explain the "enigmatic Russian soul"—from the first comments about the Russian character in the reports of foreign ambassadors received by Yaroslav the Wise in tenth-century Kiev, to numerous international conferences, publications, and debates today.

However, the modern dictionary definition of "mentality" as "a habitual or characteristic mental attitude, an outlook, a mind-set, that determines how you will interpret and respond to situations," cannot be applied to Russia. The minds of the Russians have been set and broken so many times during all the reforms, wars, and social experiments in Russian history, that old values, without having had enough time to become fully established, were overtaken by new value systems, only for these to be destroyed in turn.

"It can take several months, sometimes weeks, to change the political regime; decades to reform the national economy; but centuries to change the national culture," writes Tatyana Zaslavskaya.

The social transformations in Russia—be they Peter the Great's "Westernization" of the country and reform of the calendar, Lenin's postrevolutionary industrialization plan, or *perestroika* and the liberalization of the 1990s— have always come as bursts of drastic measures, based on decisions from the top. In the twentieth century alone the Russian system of values has been changed at least twice—in 1917 and in the 1990s. It would be simplistic, therefore, to describe one rigid framework of Russian beliefs, morals, and attitudes.

If you cut the Russian mentality pie you will find layers of Orthodox Christian values, the moral code of the "Builder of Communism," the influx of Western culture during *perestroika*, and the recent strengthening of the national idea.

The philosopher Ivan Ilyin succinctly described the factors that influenced Russian mentality: "For centuries the Russian character was built by monasteries and armies, state governance, and the family unit. It created incredible role models of heroes, who would uniquely combine freedom and discipline." Consideration of each of those elements in more detail might help to shed light on the Russian national character.

ATTITUDES TOWARD AUTHORITY

"Bez tsarya v golove"—"without a tsar in his head"—is a Russian saying about somebody who does not know what he is doing. Or, rather, who

does not listen to the tsar telling him what to do.

In the nineteenth century even Russian liberals cited autocracy as one of three foundation stones of the Russian state, together with spirituality and a communal spirit. The tradition of a powerful leader, be it a tsar or a president, is still strong in Russia today.

Although the Russian president often repeats that he would like the public to see him as a person they have hired for the job, opinion polls show that he is primarily regarded as a father figure, as somebody who provides material benefits and who disciplines or punishes corrupt civil servants and thieving oligarchs.

Unfortunately, the Russian autocratic tradition was often based on the rule of fear, as in the reigns of Ivan the Terrible or Peter the Great. The pervasiveness and intensity of fear reached its nadir during the bloody regime of Joseph Stalin, and this fear and the necessity to obey orders created a fundamental contradiction in the Russian attitude to authority.

"A peasant will listen to what the master has to say, but will do it his own way," says a Russian proverb.

"The political regimes change, leaders with different temperaments and intentions come to power, political systems get replaced, and yet there is one thing, that remains constant in Russia: the power is always "them," and the people are always "us," writes the Russian philosopher Shapovalov.

These contrasting attitudes, respect for and support of the top "father figure" and total disrespect for law and authority, are yet another Russian contradiction.

SOCIAL JUSTICE

In the 1930s around 80 percent of Russians were still working on the land, though the industrialization plan of the Communist government in the 1920s led to the migration of millions of peasants into urban areas. Those new city dwellers brought with them the agrarian values of the *obshchina*, the village commune, historically the core of Russian peasant life. The head of the *obshchina* symbolized the patriarchal power of the family head. He controlled the communal purse and was the ultimate authority and decision maker. Members of the *obshchina* had to be prepared to help each other in order to survive, harvest together, and fulfil their social roles dutifully. Cooperation and reciprocity were the key values of the commune. Everything in the *obshchina*, from land to money, was divided between the members on the principles of social equality and established order. Anybody who wanted to break out of his allocated role, have his own way, or earn more was disapproved of by the members of the commune.

As a result of the traditional Russian communal spirit, and seventy years of building the "classless society of Communism, where all people would be brethren," the principle of social justice and equality has been ingrained in public consciousness.

All for One and One for All

A Russian student, sharing a room with two English students in a hostel in St. Petersburg, was horrified when one of the English girls brought herself a glass of milk and a bun from the downstairs cafeteria.

"How could she do that?" asked the Russian student, indignantly.

"But you didn't ask her to bring you a bun," commented the other English student.

"I am not at all hungry, as a matter of fact, but that's not the point! She should have thought about you and me, not just about herself!" was the reply.

Every child in Russia learns Pushkin's fairy tale about the fisherman, his wicked wife, and the gold fish. A gold fish, caught by a fisherman, grants him and his wife three wishes. Each wish of the fisherman's wife is a request for higher status and a bigger home. The gold fish fulfills her desires, but up to a limit. When she aims too high, she is sent back to her hut and to the broken trough. This tale, sparkling with Pushkin's wonderful gift of storytelling, also reminds a Russian, "Don't try to rise above your peers. Don't aim too high, or you will lose everything."

Nowadays the principle of social justice manifests itself in nostalgia for the minimum social guarantees for all of the Soviet era and open disapproval of those who are richer and more successful. The political Party of Social Justice, which recently merged with another influential party, the Party of Pensioners, has a significant number of supporters.

ATTITUDES TOWARD THE INDIVIDUAL

"The Westernizing tradition, which considers the rights of the individual as fundamental, has for many centuries been weaker in Russia than the Slavophile one, which accepts authoritarian government and severe restrictions on human rights," comments Professor German Diligensky.

There is no direct equivalent of the word "privacy" in Russian. The notion is translated descriptively as "necessity of a private space," or as "solitude or seclusion." The Russian communal way of living, reincarnated in the Soviet party cells and the work units of an industrial plant, is based on the idea of sacrificing individual aspirations for the sake of a common cause: building Communism, or winning the war. A man becomes a cog in the state machine, and the worth of an individual life is significantly diminished.

"The death of one person is tragic, the death of a million is a statistic," is a remark attributed to Stalin. Historians now wonder whether 20 million is the final number of victims who perished in Stalin's Gulag camps, or whether the figure is not significantly higher. Often, to create space for newcomers, the guards would not allow prisoners to wear warm clothes in the freezing Siberian temperature, or would run hundreds of convicts into the icy water. Most of the prisoners would die of pneumonia and the statistics recorded these as "deaths from natural causes."

The recent shocking figure of 27 million Russians who gave their lives in fighting Nazism in the Second World War is the true price of the battlefield victories of the Soviet Army. "I had seen so many deaths that I did not want to write about the war after the victory. All I wanted was to forget it," wrote Daniil Granin, the prominent Russian writer often called "the consciousness of the nation."

Almost every family in Russia has a memory of family members or friends arrested during Soviet times for being "politically unreliable," and preserves its own tragic war history.

Individual initiative and freedom of expression were severely suppressed under Communism. Even pupils expressing their own thoughts in school essays were punished with bad marks. Individual creativity though, bursting to be let out, was often channeled into technical invention. The Russian tradition of invention, craftsmanship, and technical ingenuity is well-known. The story about "Levsha," the serf craftsman who shod a flea, is a classic, studied in the school curriculum.

NASHE—NE MOJE (OURS DOES NOT MEAN MINE)

There is another important aspect of communal living, often disregarded: the land that the serfs were working on was not their property. The results of their work were taken away, and they did not care for the land or the buildings on it.

Maybe that's why in Russian villages and small towns away from the tourist routes, the buildings are in such a neglected state, built on the off chance of just about lasting or, as Russians would say, *na avos*.

In the Soviet era the notion of private property was limited to consumer goods in a state-owned apartment and a *dacha*, a country house, or an allotment. No surprise then, that it is from the *dacha* that the transformation of the attitude to private property began: if you go down the Rublevskoje highway out of Moscow, you will see the "palaces" of the New Russians along the road advertising their wealth.

NATIONAL PRIDE

During the ardent debates and discussions of the parliamentary election campaign, there is one topic all the candidates agree upon. Practically all the parties have a patriotic slogan in their campaign, accepting that this is a definite winner.

The love of *Rodina* (the Motherland) has always given Russians inspiration and strength. In the absence of a common goal after the collapse of the Communism, the national idea has become a uniting ideology, key to the future development and security of the country. Sixty percent of the population welcomed the return of the music of the national anthem of the USSR as the Russian national anthem, and the double-headed eagle, symbol of tsarist Russia before the revolution, as the national emblem.

Russian military history has always been a source of national pride, reflected in the names of the greatest military victories—the Patriotic War of 1812, the Great Patriotic War of 1941–45. An inherent sense of justice, self-sacrifice, courage, and discipline are traditional Russian military values. The fact that patriotic films about Russian military bravery and discipline in bygone and in present times, be it protecting the borders, fighting terrorism, or in Chechnya, are shown almost weekly on national television is a vivid testimony of the resurgence of this spirit today.

It would be wrong, however, to say that an aggressive, militaristic spirit is "in the Russian blood." In medieval times, when the year was peaceful, the chronicler would often leave a space against that year and write nothing, only noting the battles and the conflicts when they occurred. Hence the early history of Russia often reads as a history of war and aggression, with no mention of the peaceful years.

Russia's relative self-isolation and massive territory needed protection from its neighbors. In the postwar years the Soviet population lived by the slogan "We'll survive any hardships as long as there is no war." Russian military strength provided additional security and an all-important boost for morale and productivity.

There is a worrying tendency in the present surge of Russian patriotism, however. In 2003 the slogan "Russia for the Russians" was supported by about 15 percent of the population. In 2006 this figure was more than 50 percent. Sociologists see this as a response to poverty and discontent with the steady flow of "working migrants" from the former Soviet republics. Official figures showing that 90 percent of all crimes are committed by migrants, and that migrants now hold the majority of low-paid jobs, taking them away from Russians, only fuel these negative feelings.

RESPONDING TO CHANGE

Every society, like every individual, develops its own mechanism of adaptation to times of social transformation and instability. In the 1990s, the breakup of the Communist system led to the bizarre transformation of some values and to the appearance of new ones.

The diminished role of the "father figure" state made many people feel like abandoned children—hence the symptoms of frustration at being cheated and neglected. The older generation retreated into passiveness, not ready to accept the new freedoms or the idea of property rights. After seventy years in an egalitarian society, for many adjusting to the idea of "ownership" and, more importantly, to the responsibility that comes with it, proved a burden too heavy to bear.

There is no surprise that criminality flourished at the beginning of the 1990s. Though based on violence and deceit, organized crime has its own system of values, involving total obedience within the group and adherence to a strict clan hierarchy. Wasn't this phenomenon not merely an outcry against unstable times, but also a sinister version of the Russian *obshchina* mentality, the rule of fear, and the submission of individuality?

The time of hope, poverty, freedom, and complete confusion at the beginning of the 1990s was replaced by disappointment with the reform's lack of results, loss of faith in the government, and acceptance of overwhelming corruption at all levels of power as a fact of everyday life. All these factors have contributed to worrying tendencies in present-day Russian society: national pride sometimes turns to extremism, exasperation is replaced by aggressiveness, and loss of hope leads to total passivity. According to a recent sociological survey, 43 percent of the Russian population will vote for the presidential candidate nominated by the president.

However, it would be wrong to paint a totally gloomy picture. The individualistic, pragmatic approach to life, born in the capitalist Russia of the nineteenth century, got a new boost with the change to a market economy in the 1990s. The younger generation, brought up without the

Soviet legacy, has learned to be self-reliant and independent. "One of our most European features is that we are now putting 'me' before 'we,'" was the comment of a young student on a Moscow street in an interview aired on an American TV channel.

The new post-Soviet generation, while striving for independent thinking, embracing new Western technologies, traveling the world, and making their own judgment of right and wrong, still retains a core Russian value, one that is at the heart of Russian life: the importance of family.

THE FAMILY UNIT

Surveys and public opinion polls are an integral part of everyday life in Russia: reaction to changes in the economy, politics, and public life are monitored almost daily by private and state institutions, international foundations, and NGOs.

A survey conducted in St. Petersburg in 2005 invited the public to rate seven major life values. According to the poll results, the first three were: family (67 percent), health (57 percent), and friends (37 percent). They were followed by: interesting job (34 percent), money (31 percent), social justice (29 percent), and faith (16 percent). Every sociologist knows that the results of a poll often depend on the way the questions are asked. However, the question: What are you particularly proud of in your life?" is not ambivalent. The most common answer to this question, asked by

the Levada Research Center across Russia, was:
"I am most proud of being (or becoming) a
father/mother."

Children

The Russian attitude to children can be summed
up in two "Ks": *Kormit i kutat* (feed and wrap up
warm). Parents protect, sometimes overprotect,
their children. The common wisdom is "Our lives
were hard, at least our children will live better . . ."
Children are a constant source of pride: their
academic, sports, or musical
achievements are gladly discussed and
demonstrated. Russians will more
readily spend money on their
offspring's education and travels than
on themselves. Russian children, on
leaving the nest, keep a lifelong bond
with their parents.

Once a Child, Always a Child

The deputy head of the counseling service in
Moscow, talking about the main problems people
come to them with, comments: "Twenty-five
percent of our clients come to us because they are
worried about their children—their apathy,
anxiousness, or reticence. And we are talking
about the problems of children of all ages—aged
from ten to fifty."

It is not surprising, however, that in times of social instability and transformation the core values are the first to crack: according to recent statistics, there are 750,000 orphans in Russia and every third child is born out of wedlock, with 20 percent of those not knowing who their father is.

Attitudes Toward the Older Generation

At the time of the collapse of the Soviet system, when most retirees lost their savings, those who had extended family relied on them for financial support. Those who did not could be seen begging or selling cigarettes and newspapers in the street.

There is a strong tradition of duty and respect for the elderly. Every year, on May 9, Victory Day, the war veterans parade through the streets and talk to children at schools. The Soviet tradition of celebrating the role of the veterans, publicly acknowledging their bravery and wisdom, is still kept today, though with the passage of time it becomes harder to find the veterans for those meetings. With the dramatic difference in life expectancy between men (fifty-eight) and women (seventy-three), it is not surprising that attitudes to older people means primarily the attitude to *babushka,* or granny.

There is a typical image of the "granny council" gathering on the benches outside their apartments and village houses to gossip and comment on everybody walking their way. These granny councils are a Russian take on "neighborhood watch." As every passerby is scrutinized and discussed, it can be a great deterrent for robbers.

One of many contradictions of Russian society is that though their seniors are respected in the family hierarchy, and the *babushka* is often the one who brings up the grandchildren and is considered the hearth keeper, the generation gap between the post-Soviet generation and the granny, who was brought up in the rigidity of the Soviet system, is enormous.

ATTITUDES TOWARD WOMEN

What is your image of a Russian woman? A long-legged blonde model, a middle-aged customs officer in a khaki uniform with dyed red hair, or a downtrodden *babushka* selling cigarettes by the entrance to the Moscow metro? The attitude toward women encapsulates the contradictory nature of modern Russian values.

Flirtatiousness and gallantry toward women in Russia (opening the door, helping her put on her coat, or with heavy bags) might leave even the most seasoned American female executive at a loss. Women are referred to as the weaker sex, to be admired, loved, and complimented. Don't be surprised if the women in the rush-hour metro look as if they are ready for the theater—the grayness of the Soviet era has been replaced by the open sensuality of teenage girls and the groomed perfection of businesswomen.

A mega-successful Russian chain of designer

lingerie shops called "The Wild Orchid" promotes the image of "a dream Russian woman"—sensual and smart, who knows her beauty and knows her worth. According to the PR director of the chain, women of all ages, from the teenage daughters of wealthy parents to women in their late forties, eagerly leave "small" fortunes in their shops.

And yet the model of Russian femininity is strength and independence. The Russian woman is the type who will, according to the Russian poet Nekrasov, "stop a horse in its jump, run into a burning house . . . " She is a mother, and the keeper of family traditions.

In Soviet times the working woman was praised as an equal builder of Communism. When so many men perished in Stalin's purges and in the war, Russian women became the backbone of society.

As the homemaker, the Russian woman, if she is one of the 85 percent who cannot afford domestic help, still has a clearly defined role at home. Help around the house by the husband is an exception rather than a rule.

A Woman's World

When a young Russian woman in Moscow saw her English husband clearing the dishes and washing up for the first time, she got quite upset: "Are you doing this to criticize me and show me the standard I should achieve while clearing up?" she demanded from her bewildered husband.

SPIRITUALITY

For over a thousand years the Russian Orthodox Church played an important role in Russian history. It united the Russian princes in the age of feudal strife; it gave the people comfort at the time of the Tatar invasions; it developed art, blessed soldiers before battles, and fostered education.

In the Russian Orthodox tradition all one can do is hope; one should be humble and patient, accept destiny with humility, and wait to enter into the Kingdom of God. In 1917 the Bolsheviks adapted Orthodox values to the new religion of Communism, only now one was working for the advent of World Communism, for a "brighter future" and happiness on earth, not in heaven. The icons were replaced by portraits of Marx and Lenin, with the later addition of Stalin and other leaders; the prayers, by citations from the works of Marx, Lenin, and later by other Soviet party leaders. Twelve commandments were carefully woven into the "Moral Code of the Builder of Communism." The values of the Russian Orthodox Church—patience, humility, and mutual assistance—were ideally suited for the hardworking collectives of the "builders of Communism."

It comes as no surprise that churches and monasteries were barbarically destroyed in the 1920s and '30s, and priests were arrested, sent to camps, or murdered:

two official religions in the country of Bolshevism could not compete.

In 1941, in order to strengthen the spirit of the nation, Stalin enlisted the Orthodox Church for help. He ordered the release of numerous priests from prisons and camps, reopened churches for services, and addressed the nation as "brethren and sisters," not comrades. In the last years of socialist stagnation, however, the churches were half empty, attended only by *babushkas* and tourists. After the aggressive atheism of the Soviet years, the present surge of religious interest in Russia puzzles many foreigners.

According to research conducted by the Levada Analytic Center in 1991, 61 percent of the population considered themselves atheists, and 31 percent Russian Orthodox. In 1995 the proportion of the population considering themselves Russian Orthodox had doubled to around 60 percent. How could this have happened in just four years?

The collapse of the Soviet Union and the discrediting of Soviet ideology created a vacuum of faith: if there were to be no Communist paradise ahead, what could people believe in? At first the vacuum was filled by numerous American sects, and by magicians and con artists claiming enormous extrasensory powers; but by the middle of the 1990s the majority of the population had turned to Orthodox Christianity. With its chanting, choral music, myrrh aromas, and ornate churches, the Russian Orthodox faith appeals to the subconscious, to the emotional side of our nature, providing relief and hope.

The Easter vigil mass (*vsenoshnaja*) is transmitted on national TV from Christ the Savior Cathedral, with the president and the mayor of Moscow present. Note that the Easter mass involves four hours of standing.

The Cathedral of Christ the Savior

The newly restored Cathedral of Christ the Savior in Moscow is a symbol of Russia's spiritual revival. The cathedral was built in 1881 to commemorate the Russian victory over the Napoleonic army in the Great Patriotic war of 1812. In 1931 Stalin decided to destroy the cathedral and replace it with a new "temple"—a Palace of the Soviets with a colossal 100-meter tall statue of Lenin on top. The cathedral was blown up and the site cleared for the proposed palace. However, due to numerous technical difficulties the building was never actually constructed, and the foundations for the palace were turned into a heated public swimming pool, which was in use for several decades. In 1995 the Russian Orthodox Church asked the government to allow the restoration of the cathedral. A public fund was set up to raise money for the costly project, and the heavy bronze doors of the enormous, lavish building opened again in August 2000.

If you have a chance, try to attend a Sunday service. You will see all strata of society gathered there—retirees and crew-cut youths in leather jackets, middle-aged women, and skinny teenagers.

You don't have to be present for the whole service, but respect the basic rules: enter and leave quietly. Women should wear head scarves; men take their hats off as they enter the cathedral.

OPTIMISTIC FATALISM

In a poll conducted in St. Petersburg in 2000, out of forty-two proverbs offered 83.6 percent of respondents singled out as their favorite, "Whatever is done is done for the better." These words are the essence of what is often called Russian "optimistic fatalism," the attitude that life just carries on by itself.

Although there is an optimistic "things will get better somehow" element to it, the responsibility for change is subconsciously passed to an outside agency—to destiny, to luck, or to the government. This is the unsurprising result of centuries of repressed individualism and commands from the top. It is encouraging, therefore, that the outlook of the younger generation is becoming more proactive.

SUPERSTITIONS

In the twenty-first century world one wouldn't expect a tiny superstition to turn into an international diplomatic incident. And yet that is

Be a Participant...

"Whether we want a house, dream of a parachute jump or a Lamborghini, we always find hundreds of reasons for our own lack of action: we don't want a bigger house because a small one is easier to clean; parachute jumping is not possible because of the weather, and a Lamborghini will break down after two miles on the Russian roads. We wish each other happiness, health, and prosperity as abstract notions, without thinking what steps we should take to achieve them ... Be a participant in your own dream, not just a dreamer!"

From an article in a leading Russian magazine targeted at women under forty.

exactly what could happen if a political or a business leader, wishing to welcome his Russian counterpart, were to extend his open palm as soon as he opened the door. He might be very surprised to receive a concerned frown from his Russian guest, as he would not have realized that he had broken the unspoken rule: never shake hands across the threshold—this brings bad luck. Welcome to the invisible world of Russian superstitions.

Pagan roots, the magical beliefs of the indigenous minorities in Siberia, and the Russian love of all things mystical have created a set of superstitions that give people extra hope when things are not going well and explain misfortune in the darker days.

So, when in Russia, don't bring misfortune on yourself by: shaking hands across the porch, whistling in the house, returning for something you have forgotten after you have left the house, leaving an empty bottle on the table, or boasting about your future success. Expect fortune to follow you if: you have sat in silence for a moment before setting out on a journey, married in the rain, or sat between two people with the same name. Oh, and don't buy any baby presents before the baby is born, or tell somebody about your wish—it will not come true! If you are exhausted just reading about this, think what it is like living with it on a daily basis.

EMOTIONS—MEASURING THE IMMEASURABLE

Most researchers of the "enigmatic Russian soul" seem to agree on one thing: while Western culture is often based on rational decisions and planning, Russian culture is based on emotional response and spontaneity. Often where the Westerner says "I think," a Russian would say "I feel." The Russian language is the world's richest in words describing emotions. The whole world admires the feelings expressed in the books of Pushkin, Tolstoy, Dostoyevsky, Turgenev, and Chekhov.

Many things in Russian life appeal to the irrational. The Russian Orthodox religion, based on chanting and methodical movements, affects the spirit, not the mind; great distances and long journeys lead to philosophical, abstract discussions; even vodka drinking is often cited as a way of detachment from everyday life.

"We cannot see this reality with our eyes, but we perceive it within our minds," is an Orthodox religious saying. This ability to move away from everyday hardships and practicalities into the surreal world of pure emotions—instant joy, profound sorrow, deep soul searching—is always surprising to foreigners.

The Russians are often called a gloomy, melancholic nation. In the film *Moscow on the Hudson* a Russian musician, defecting to the States in the 1970s, explains it to his American friend: "Everybody in Russia loves his misery. We haven't got much else, but each one will love his own misery, watch it grow, and look after it—it is his own misery after all!"

One can attribute this to the tragic history of long suffering, the harsh climate, or even to the five-tone minor melodies of Russian folk songs, but the bottom line remains the same—moaning is a national pastime. But then, if the decision to sort out one's troubles always lies with somebody else, what else can one do?

Peter the Great, we have seen, decided to sort out Russian moodiness in a dramatic way. He established the "*vseshutejshiy sobor*," the academy of merriment and theater, and during the New Year celebrations even sent out the merriment police to check the level of enjoyment in the homes of the *boyars*.

I PITY HIM, SO I LOVE HIM

The introduction of jury service following the recent judicial reforms in Russia has led to an unexpected result: a significant increase in acquittals. The jury, with a female majority, tends to acquit even in the face of hard evidence, appealing to the Russian principles of compassion and forgiveness. "He pities me" and "he loves me" are often synonymous in Russian literature.

In 2005 one of the national magazines for female readers ran an article questioning whether compassion was a necessary virtue in Russian society today. The gist was that compassion as a traditional Russian value is obsolete—it humiliates both those who are felt sorry for and those who sympathize. This is particularly relevant to women whose husbands are alcoholics, drug addicts, or constant pessimists. These men feel cocooned by compassion, and do not make any attempt to break out of the cocoon and change their lives for the better. The wives who show compassion feel guilt and an increasing burden of duty, but their role of the Mother–Savior gives them a sense of direction and a purpose to live.

"Stop feeling sorry for a grown-up person who behaves like an infant," suggests the magazine. "The person you feel sorry for should learn to be responsible for himself. The role of a nanny is unhealthy. It is your duty to start thinking about your needs, to love yourself and respect yourself." One might agree or disagree with this statement, but the article highlights the attempt to break away from the tradition of martyrdom and self-sacrifice and establish the rights of a self-conscious individual, with his or her own needs and powers of decision making.

PORTRAIT OF A RUSSIAN

Recently the Levada Center ran a poll on how Russians perceive themselves. According to this, the Russians see themselves as: "open hearted and kind, hospitable, lazy and irresponsible, unpragmatic, and patient to the point of humiliation."

This portrait mirrors the classic Russian folk tale hero, Yemelya, who is lovable and gullible, unlike his smart elder brothers; he does not work hard, but gets what he wants in the end.

Indeed, if one looks at Russian history, the development of such a character becomes clear. What was the point of working hard if somebody (a Tatar, a tsar, or a Soviet state) would take away the results of your work anyway? And maybe it was easier to pretend to be naive and unpragmatic in order to survive? The regime of fear was overcome by the rule of resourcefulness. "A Russian is smart, but pretends to be a fool," wrote the Russian historian Kluchevsky.

This portrait lacks one significant feature not mentioned by the respondents at all: Russian resilience.

RESLIENCE

In 1998 the Russian ruble fell five times overnight and wiped out the newly emerging middle class. What would you do if your national currency collapsed, taking your savings down with it? Or if prices were to rise twenty-six times in one year? And yet the majority of Russians continued working, loving, and laughing.

The national ability to overcome hardships has been proved by history. As the words of a modern Russian pop song have it, "We Russians will get up from our knees despite everything!"

FESTIVALS & CUSTOMS

NATIONAL HOLIDAYS AND FESTIVALS

The Russian year is full of celebrations, which are a mixture of the Soviet legacy, holidays introduced after independence, and the revival of Orthodox festivities. State holidays, often marked red in Russian calendars, are the official days off.

National Holidays

New Year	January 1–2
Russian Orthodox Christmas	January 7
Day of the Defender of the Motherland	February 23
Women's Day	March 8
Spring and Labor Day	May 1–2
Victory Day	May 9
Independence Day	June 12
National Unity Day	November 4

January 1: New Year's Day

This, according to a recent survey, is the Russians' favorite holiday. As New Year's Day is the only holiday not affected by politics or religion, this is not surprising.

The festive celebrations begin with decorating the tree—in Russia it's a New Year tree, not a Christmas tree. The presents are brought by Ded Moroz (Father Frost), a version of Santa Claus, and Snegurochka, his blonde Snow Maiden granddaughter. (Nobody seems to question the fact of Ded Moroz's unmarried state.)

There is a saying that a person will spend the year in the same way as he has welcomed it in. Therefore, the tradition is to have a big celebration, with fireworks and fanfare, and to party through the night with enthusiasm.

It is hard to believe, but even this celebration is an example of the Tsar's imposed will. In December 1699, Russia was in the year 7208, calculated from the birth of the world. Peter the Great at that time decided to give Russia a totally new calendar, in line with that of Europe, and announced that the next year would be 1700. Massive parties and celebrations were decreed, and the "merriment police" were authorized to break into people's houses to check whether they were indeed celebrating. Those who weren't (or, maybe, who were still in shock, learning to accept the new time frame) were severely punished.

Off Season
If you should miss the New Year celebration, there is another chance to get a present from Ded Moroz. June is the best time to see him, while he is in Russia, and not visiting Santa Claus in Finland for a joint winter celebration. It's official: Ded Moroz resides in Veliky Ustug, a small town in the Vologda Oblast of northwest Russia, in a carved wooden palace. He has his own post office, orchestra, newspapers and magazines, and, of course, a sleigh. His first passport, according to the official records, was issued on January 1, 1048.

January 7: Orthodox Christmas
Celebration of Orthodox Christmas was forbidden under the Soviet regime, and was resurrected officially only in 1992. The Russian Orthodox Church still uses the old Julian calendar; therefore, Christmas falls on January 7, thirteen days after the Christmas celebrations in Europe. At midnight the Orthodox churches start their divine service with choral chanting. The first traditional dish on Christmas Eve is *kutya* (a sweet soup made with poppy seeds, honey, nuts, and barley). All dishes should be meatless.

February 23: Day of the Defender of the Motherland (Former Red Army Day)
Due to the principle of conscription, 90 percent of men served at some point in the Soviet Army—or at least were supposed to do so. In the absence of

Father's Day, February 23 developed into a male celebration. Most women give presents to their male relatives and friends, and expect reciprocation on Women's Day, March 8.

March 8: International Women's Day

Beware of the price of flowers on this day. It doubles, according to the Moscow newspapers. You will hardly see a woman on the street without tulips or roses. Men present chocolate, flowers, and small gifts to their wives, mothers, daughters, sisters, and female friends and colleagues. Ironically, as the men want to celebrate as well, the women still end up doing the cooking!

Easter

The preparations for Easter, the biggest event in the Russian Orthodox calendar, start well in advance. With the upsurge of religion in the country many people observe Lent and fast. In 2007 an alternative Lenten menu was introduced on planes and trains in Russia, so if you travel on the Trans-Siberian express you can follow the Russian-style observance. Three days before Easter is Clean Thursday, when everything should be thoroughly cleaned at home.

For many people the celebration continues with a church service on Saturday evening. It starts at 11:30 p.m., and lasts until 4:00 a.m. In recent years the service has been broadcast on television and attended by political leaders.

The Orthodox priest greets the congregation

with the words, "Christ is risen!" and the reply, in chorus, is "Indeed He is risen!" With these words people exchange a triple kiss.

During the day people visit their relatives and close friends and present them with *paskhas* (Easter cakes) and painted hard-boiled eggs. The Russian tradition of Easter egg fights is similar to the Greek one. Before the festive dinner everyone tries to hit their neighbor's egg and break the shell. The person whose eggshell is left intact will have the most luck throughout the year.

May 1: Festival of Spring (Former Labor Day)
This day is a legacy of Soviet times, when it was one of the greatest holidays of the year, with grandiose parades and propaganda banners. Although it is no longer celebrated as International Worker's Solidarity Day, it still retains its festive spirit, with people going to parks and the countryside for barbecues and picnic celebrations. May 2 is also a day off.

May 9: Victory Day
For Russians this is the day the Great Patriotic War against Nazi Germany ended in 1945, a day to remember the millions who died in the struggle, and to honor the veterans. The veterans (fewer every year) wear their uniforms and medals for the day, meeting the remaining "*odnopolchane,*" wartime friends, in the parks. Big

military parades are held, and wreaths are put on the Tomb of the Unknown Soldier.

June 12: Independence Day (Russia Day)

On this day in 1990 the Russian parliament formally declared the independence of the Russian Federation. The holiday was established by President Yeltsin in 1991, and has been officially recognized ever since.

November 4: National Unity Day

November has always been a turbulent month in Russian history, and the juggling of the November holidays in the last decade reflects this.

For almost seventy years the Soviet Union celebrated Great October Socialist Revolution Day on November 7 (or October 25 old style), the day of the Bolshevik uprising in St. Petersburg in 1917. Once a great Soviet holiday, with two days off, it lost its political significance after the collapse of the Soviet system. The system has gone, but many still cling to the custom. One can still see some Communist retirees marching with red flags and banners on that day, demonstrating for the restoration of the "stability of the good old days." The day was diplomatically renamed "National Accord and Reconciliation Day" after the fall of the Soviet Union.

In 2005 a new November celebration was created—according to some observers to counterbalance those nostalgic Soviet-style demonstrations. It commemorates the expulsion of the Polish-Lithuanian occupying force from Moscow in November 1612. Following the Russian proverb that "all things new are the well forgotten old ones," National Unity Day is a resurrection of a public holiday held in Russia on October 22 (old style) from 1649 untill 1917.

In explaining the significance of the new holiday, Duma Speaker Boris Gryzlov characterized it as a "patriotic holiday [celebrating] Russia's military glory, which also serves as a reminder of the dangers and unacceptability of confrontation within society," according to the Russian Web site "strana.ru."

However, according to a poll conducted by the Levada Center in October 2004 among 1,600 Russian citizens in forty-six regions, just 6 percent approved of the introduction of the new holiday, while 36 percent disapproved of it and said they would prefer to continue observing National Accord and Reconciliation Day (Day of the Great October Socialist Revolution). Approximately 24 percent said they did not care which holiday they celebrated, so long as they got a day off.

"WORKING" HOLIDAYS AND FESTIVALS

Apart from the state holidays, there are a number of "public holidays" that are regular working days for government offices, shops, and companies, but a great excuse to have a party. In addition to these, the various religious holidays bring their own rituals and joys. Only the most important are mentioned here.

January 13: Old New Year's Day

Before 1917 Russia, following the Julian calendar, was thirteen days behind the rest of the world. However, even though the official calendar was switched in 1917, many people refused to change their habits and continued to celebrate New Year as before. As a result, there are two New Year celebrations in Russia. The celebrations for the Old New Year are not held on such a grand scale as those on January 1, and it is not a day off work.

January 19: *Kreshenije* (Baptism)

On this day the Orthodox Church remembers the baptism of Jesus by John in the Jordan River. Solemn religious processions to consecrate rivers, springs, and wells take place all over Russia. Priests immerse a cross in the water through a hole in the ice. After the service believers consecrate their own houses with sacred water. One can only admire the courage of those who plunge into icy water to be baptized, despite the freezing January temperatures.

Well Wishes

A Russian card for businessmen during the celebration of Baptism: "This is the day when the Angel is sitting on your shoulder, baptizing your new enterprise. Good luck in your negotiations!"

January 25: Tatayana's Day, or Students' Day

In 1775, on the day of Maiden Tatiana the Martyr, the Russian Empress Elizabeth Petrovna signed a decree, "On the foundation of Moscow University." In the eighteenth and nineteenth centuries this day was celebrated as Day of the Foundation of Moscow University, but in the second half of the nineteenth century it had already become a holiday for all universities and students. All present and former students enjoy the day, which is a celebration of the carefree times of youth.

February 14: St. Valentine's Day

This is a new, post-Soviet holiday, enjoyed by the younger generation and greetings-card manufacturers alike.

Maslenitsa (Shrovetide)

The holiday of welcoming spring and saying farewell to the frosts of winter is celebrated on a large scale, Russian-style. Unlike Shrove Tuesday, it lasts for a whole week and culminates on Shrove Sunday, with carnivals, bonfires, snow fortress fights, and troika sleigh rides. Like Shrove Tuesday, it does involve pancakes. "There's no Shrovetide without pancakes, and no birthday party without pies," says a Russian proverb. The tradition stems from the pagan cult of the sun, and the symbolic round, golden pancakes are served with butter, caviar, sour cream—treats to remember, as Shrovetide is the last week before the seven weeks of Lent.

April 1: Fool's Day

The day to play pranks and practical jokes on people is well established in Russia. Several years ago the newspaper *Komsomolskaya Pravda* reported in its April 1 issue that a frozen mammoth calf had been found in Chukotka, and that it had been revived and taken to a Moscow zoo. A schoolteacher from Siberia, not realizing that this was a practical joke, organized an excursion for a group of pupils to see it, involving a six-hour flight. She had quite a row with the zoo administration!

Holy Trinity

Observed on the fiftieth day after Easter, Trinity is one of the most important religious holidays, but has only recently become a state celebration. It is a day when people celebrate a new life through decorating their houses and apartments with grass and wildflowers. Parents' Saturday before Trinity is a day of commemoration of relatives who have passed away.

September 1: Day of Knowledge

On the first day of the academic year in every school well-dressed pupils bring flowers for their teachers. The first-year children gather for the inauguration assembly in the schoolyard, at which a first-year girl is carried on the shoulder of a graduating student, ringing the first bell, opening the Road to Knowledge.

"PROFESSIONAL" HOLIDAYS

If this extensive list of official, public, and religious holidays is not enough, there are also holidays celebrating particular professions. There is Russian Press Day on January 13; Firefighters' Day on April 30; Librarians' Day on May 27; Border Guards' Day on May 28; Post Office Workers' Day on July 9; . . . it seems as though every year another profession is added.

Astronauts' Day is one of the most popular professional holidays, despite the fact that members of this profession can be counted in hundreds rather than thousands. It is celebrated every April 12 to commemorate the first manned Earth orbit on that day in 1962.

The commemoration ceremony starts in the city of Korolyov, near Yuri Gagarin's statue. The participants then proceed under police escort to Red Square for a visit to Gagarin's grave in the Kremlin Wall Necropolis, and continue to Cosmonauts Alley, near the Monument to the Conquerors of Space.

Much is made of birthday celebrations in Russia. They are celebrated both at home and in the office, with friends and colleagues. This is not all. Besides their birthday, each person has their angel's day, often celebrated as a second birthday. It is called "*Imeniny*," or "name celebration." The most popular is "*Vera, Nadezhda, Lubov*," three symbolic names translated as "Faith, Hope, Love," on September 30.

Choose Dates Carefully

With the New Year, Christmas, and Old New Year celebrations lasting until mid-January, meetings arranged in the first fortnight of the New Year are not likely to yield any tangible results.

In May, with three official days off (May 1, 2, and 9) and the beginning of the *dacha* (country house) season, many people will be away from their offices until the third week of May.

With so many holidays and celebrations, it is not surprising that Russians spend so much money on food. "The best present we should give ourselves on New Year's Eve is to stop eating so much," suggested Russian comedian Mikhail Zadornov. Quite often you will be invited to join in the party, and this is when another set of unpublished rules starts to operate. The way you behave at a party will either make or break your visit. (See Chapter 4, "Making Friends.")

chapter four

MAKING FRIENDS

Long journeys, farmers' winters, natural curiosity, and vodka are just some of the factors that contribute to the Russians' desire both to open up their souls to you and to hear your life story. After the first hour in the train, or the first drink, or the first smoking session during the lunch break, the guarded expressions will be gone, smiles will lighten the faces, and you will discover what it means to befriend a Russian.

DISTANCE AND VOLUME

In Russia people get closer to you very quickly. Literally. Personal distances are closer, be it in public transportation, standing in line, or in daily communication. The volume increases too. "I never realized you could shout at people so much," commented a bewildered English husband, when he heard his Russian wife speaking to her relatives in Russian.

If you can get used to the louder speech and closer proximity of your interlocutor, combined with patting your shoulder, leaning over to your ear, or getting even closer, to share with you a special secret about stones in the gall bladder or details of love life in the first ten minutes of a new friendship, you will have plenty of topics to discuss later. And even more to avoid.

TOPICS OF CONVERSATION
Books

In 2006 the publishing business in Russia became the fourth largest in the world and one of the top five sectors of growth in the national economy. "Computers are the strength of America, readers the strength of Russia," said Russian poet Andrey Voznesensky. Russians love books. Conversations about recent novels, philosophy, and history, or the newspaper columns, are common.

Politics

As the country goes through continuing changes in the political structure, everybody everywhere is discussing politics. So don't be surprised if the guests at the dinner table, your colleagues in the office, or *babushkas* on their neighborhood watch on the courtyard bench enter into a passionate debate on the reasons for two parties joining forces or the comments of certain MPs during a recent parliamentary session. Be careful: they will get very upset if you, a foreigner, dare to criticize the Russian government as well.

Children and Family

Russians see the progress of their children as one of their priorities, and parents will often talk about their children's achievements with pride. You will be shown their academic results, the trophy won at a recent sports competition; there will be a demonstration of musical talents and good behavior. Russians will talk not only about their children, but about their families in general. Foreigners are often surprised that Russians will discuss openly around the table the details of a family feud, problems, and wedding plans.

You Have Delighted Us Enough

"We all know how beautiful and talented your children are, Natasha. We have heard it many times before. Shall we move to the monthly report now?" was the comment of an English boss to his Russian sales manager in the Moscow office of an international company.

Baring your soul

Several toasts will lead to what appears to be extensive sentimentality or lamentation. Russians, as you will already have discovered, are quite compassionate and are often prepared to listen to and sympathize with somebody else's problems. And though in the big cities counseling services are mushrooming, in provincial towns people are often surprised to hear of the wide network of counseling services in other countries. "What are friends for, then?" is a common question.

Health and Healing

You will soon notice that health, healing, and holistic medicine are discussed in detail by everybody around you: the customs officer will discuss her headaches with her colleague while you are waiting in the passport queue, your business partner, with whom you had a heavy drinking session the night before, will cancel the morning meeting due to sudden colic, your secretary will bring the garlicky honey drops to the office for you to use as a preventative measure during the flu epidemic, and so on.

"I can't work with my Russian teacher any more," complained a British diplomat. "Every time I sneeze she stops the lesson to list the remedies I should take—from honey mixed with black radish juice to onion tincture. At least she doesn't offer them to me then and there!"

Money

Hyperinflation at the beginning of the 1990s, the collapse of pyramid financing scams, and, of course, the loss of personal savings during the crash of 1998 all make Russians very knowledgeable and experienced in the matters of banks and interest rates. Prices are often discussed, but so also are salaries, so be prepared for direct questions: "And how much do you earn?" "How much did you pay for your car?"

"And your house?" There is nothing personal there, just benign curiosity.

A Woman's Age
A woman's age is rarely mentioned. Even at a big birthday celebration the age is not referred to in the toasts. On the seventieth birthday of the first female astronaut, Valentina Tereshkova, the TV and newspapers were full of congratulations, but her age wasn't mentioned once.

HUMOR
Russians are masters of black humor. It was humor that helped people survive the hard times and gain some respite from the pressures and worries of life.

Apart from the universal jokes about infidelity and in-laws, there are also jokes reflecting the realities of Russian life: about vodka and excessive alcohol consumption, jokes about the "New Russians," corrupt militiamen (policemen) who earn their living by charging bribes, and so on.

Fines
Six o'clock in the morning. A driver is stopped by a militiaman for speeding. Militiaman: "And why were you in such a rush?" Driver, with a sigh, getting out a 100-dollar note: "I just wanted to deliver the money to you on time."

You will be expected to contribute to a joke session as well. Bear in mind that jokes have to "travel." Jokes about cricket or baseball, for example, won't be understood in Russia, as the rules are generally not known.

GENEROSITY OF SPIRIT
Your Russian friends will look after you very well, to the point that you might feel smothered. You will be shown around day and night, fed and watered, and given gifts. It will be a hard act to follow when they come to visit you.

"Come and See Me Sometime"
Sometimes a casual suggestion might be taken a little too literally. One Englishman ended up hosting a shooting party at two days' notice when, after a brief chat with a Russian businessman at a reception, he said, "My estate is great for shooting. You must come and visit me one day." The Russian, taking out his diary, replied, "Thank you. I am in the U.K. until next Tuesday, so I can come this weekend, if that's convenient. There will be seven of us—I'll bring my family, my assistants, and my bodyguards!"

VODKA
The tenth-century Kievan prince Vladimir said, "In Rus, drinking is enjoyment, and we cannot

exist without it." Vodka, cognac, champagne, wine, and beer are all drunk in Russia. But vodka is, without a doubt, the most popular drink, constituting 80 percent of all the alcohol consumed in the country.

Society sees drinking as an integral part not only of celebration and relaxation, but also of everyday life. The Russian historian William Pokhlebkin has written a history of it, analyzing cultural and social changes in Russia through vodka consumption. He claims that vodka, if drunk properly and responsibly, has little intoxicating effect. But the statistics remain grim, with the male mortality rate dropping to the age of fifty-eight, with 70 percent of all car accidents caused by drinking, and thousands dying from ersatz vodka or improperly distilled spirit.

If you can't drink, you may well be viewed with suspicion, as a person who can't be trusted. "The main advantage of becoming wealthy," said a Russian oligarch in a TV interview, "is that I can finally choose my drinking companions!"

If you want to retain the respect of your hosts and not get drunk at the same time, use your health as an excuse. You can say that you are taking medication, that you are allergic to alcohol, or your liver is enlarged to dangerous proportions already and all you are allowed to drink is herbal tea. Your refusal to drink will be understood—but you will have to listen to a lot of medical advice!

PARTIES

With the Russian tradition of hospitality and a considerable number of celebrations throughout the year, you are sure to be invited to at least one party, either at home or in a restaurant. Russian parties come in all shapes, and often score on unexpected location and spontaneity.

An English student warmly remembers a party in the city of Voronezh, where six students started the party with three hours in the *banya*, the Russian version of a sauna, followed by two hours of vodka drinking, and culminating in an ice hockey match, played on two pairs of skates with four hockey sticks and no *shaiba* (puck).

Written invitations are not common. The spontaneity and rapid changes of Russian life don't allow for long-term planning. An invitation, extended by phone or personally, generally gives three or four days' notice, though it is not unusual to be invited out for the next day.

The "Coffee Morning"

This is not a coffee morning as Westerners know it. The request "to drop in for coffee" (at home) or "to go out for coffee" (in a bar or a café) is usually spontaneous and is an invitation to have a chat. Beware, though, that if you are invited to "drop in for a quick coffee," it is most likely to be a soul-searching session, which will last well into lunch, and you are most likely to be fed—so plan your time accordingly. And note that coffee is not necessarily going to be the drink.

Tea Drinking

Russia has a strong tradition of tea drinking. Tea in Russia means black tea with a lot of sugar lumps, lemon slices, jams, cookies, sweets, and a long, relaxed conversation.

Tea was first brought to Russia from China in the sixteenth century, gained in popularity, and by the nineteenth century was being drunk by everyone—aristocrats, merchants, and peasants. The Soviet tea industry, with plantations in Krasnodar and Georgia, was the largest in the world. Nowadays, the sort of tea you drink—Chinese white-leaved or Liptons—will reveal your social status. Samovars have long been replaced by electric kettles, but the Russian tea-drinking tradition lives on.

Barbecues

Russians love the outdoors, and having a barbecue (*na shashlyky*) is their favorite activity. The atmosphere will be quite informal—think jeans and T-shirts. Such parties give a rare chance to observe Russian men's cooking skills, as grilling the meat (normally marinated overnight in red wine with spices) is considered a purely male activity. Though you'll be told "don't bring anything, just yourself," a bottle of wine will always be welcome. And if you think it is a summer activity only, think again. An American businessman still holds fond memories of a barbecue in a snowed-in wood outside Novosibirsk at minus forty degrees Celsius!

The Reception and Buffet Parties

Two decades ago receptions were regarded purely as diplomatic events, not attended by the majority of the population. Now many Russian companies hold receptions at inauguration ceremonies and product launches. But as they are a recent addition to the social repertoire, small talk and social mingling still require a lot of practicing.

For Russians, to eat standing, juggling plate and glass and holding a conversation, is not much of a celebration. One English professor, who threw a welcoming party for her group of international students in her house at Oxford, found five Russians an hour later hunched over her kitchen table, deep in conversation.

Wedding Receptions

The Russian wedding is a great event to attend as it follows many Russian traditions, old and new.

The celebrations start with laying flowers at one of the city monuments. This ceremony has its roots in the old Russian tradition of visiting "holy places" after the wedding. In the Soviet atheist state they were replaced by the visits to the monuments of Lenin and the Tomb of the Unknown Soldier. Times have changed, and in Moscow, for example, newlyweds visit Red Square, churches, and the Vorobyevy Gory hills by Moscow University for panoramic views of the city. On Saturdays in September you will see dozens of wedding parties with music, cameras, and champagne, celebrating the occasion.

The *Tamada* (toastmaster) runs the wedding. He invites the guests to speak, or even to sing; he tells jokes and recites poems. Russians often say that the success of a wedding reception depends on the toastmaster. Another wedding tradition is stealing the bride for a symbolic ransom, such as a case of champagne, a bag of money (in coins, which need to be collected quickly), or a song. So don't be surprised to see a bride with two minders in a hotel elevator—they are simply hiding her from the groom, who is finding the ransom in the hotel restaurant.

Sit-Down Dinner
The Russian word *zastolye*, which means a celebration or a banquet, can be literally translated as "at the table." It is in the process of sharing meals that friendships are forged and business deals are clinched. To attend a sit-down dinner is a skill that needs understanding and practice, be it the introduction, the toasting, the conversation, or even the consumption of the food—of which, more below.

INVITATIONS HOME
You are going to have dinner with your Russian friends at their home. You shake your host's hand as he opens the door, kiss his wife on both cheeks, and give her four yellow chrysanthemums. You drink a little, politely refuse a second helping of

food, and leave after listening to some songs, sung by the other guests. You have thoroughly enjoyed the evening, you have sent a "thank you" note, and it's a complete mystery to you why your host avoids you in the office the next day and frowns when he passes you in the corridor. What you don't realize is that your behavior the evening before was a complete breach of the unspoken protocol of hospitality in the Russian home.

Greetings

Your Russian host will be pleased to see you and shake your hand—but not across the threshold! Don't ignore this superstition: step inside and take your glove off before shaking hands. Handshakes are not obligatory, and the host may even hug you if you know him quite well. But to avoid embarrassment, don't initiate the handshake (or hug) yourself—follow the host. If he simply nods his head, that's enough for you too.

If you don't know your friend's wife well, don't hug or kiss her. Do this only if she is a long-standing friend. And don't kiss a woman or child on the forehead—this is for funerals only.

As Russians remove their shoes and change into slippers to keep their homes clean, you might be offered a pair of slippers too, especially in winter, so your socks should be presentable.

Gifts

If there are children in the family you are visiting,
they will expect you to bring something sweet.
You may also bring a bottle of wine or whiskey for
the host. Don't bring Russian vodka to the
Russians. If you are a teetotaler, an attractive tin of
good tea is a better bet. As a foreign guest, bring
something exotic, or nothing at all.

Say It With Flowers

There is no margin of error as far as the number,
color, and type of flowers you bring for the
hostess are concerned. Flowers are brought to
birthday parties, presented to sweethearts on
dates, and to teachers on the first and last days of
a school year; they are a part of political
celebrations and a way of honoring veterans. They
are a sign of joy at airport reunions and a symbol
of loss and grief at funerals. In February,
snowdrops and violets are sold on the streets as a
sign of approaching spring.

If you go to a birthday party, you must bring an
odd number of flowers—three, seven, or nine. An
even number of flowers is for funerals only.
Giving more than nine flowers indicates serious
romantic feelings and intentions. However, if you
want to splurge and present a birthday girl with as
many flowers as she has years, you might need to
subtract or add a flower to make the number odd.
Not presenting a bouquet to your girlfriend on
March 8, International Women's Day, is
considered a deadly sin.

Apart from yellow flowers, which mean separation, both red and white blooms have their own meaning. White is a symbol of innocence and is appropriate for weddings, while red flowers (especially carnations) are a symbol of victory and patriotism, and have a political connotation. Red carnations can be presented to a man on his anniversary, or to a veteran on Victory Day. In Soviet times no parade or political ceremony was complete without red carnations.

At the Table
So, you finally got through the stages of greetings, presenting gifts and flowers, and maybe changing into slippers. As aperitifs or predinner drinks are not common at Russian parties, you will be taken straight to

the dining room, where the table will be covered with more food than you can eat. And this is just for starters—literally, as these are *zakuski*, the appetizers before the main meal. They will include various salads, pickles, and cold meats. You usually help yourself—and if you take it, you should eat it.

A Russian housewife will think that her guests are unhappy if they don't eat well, and eat again, and again. Overfeeding the guests is a national tradition, exacerbated by the fact that refusing food is considered to be rude.

When you finally get to desserts, which are served at the same time as tea or coffee, you will hardly be able to speak. You will also be expected to toast the hosts, friendship, and the cooking skills of the hostess before departing. And, if the evening goes well, you'll be invited to join in the singing too. An Englishman attending a wedding in Russia had to survive the drunken wrath of a fellow guest, who did not believe him when he said that he didn't know any of the traditional Russian songs the man was urging him to sing!

Toasting

Russians are enthusiastic toasters, and a party is not a celebration without a series of toasts. This follows a strict set of rules. The host usually makes the first toast in honor of the guest. The second toast is usually made to the parents during a birthday or anniversary, or to friendship at a corporate banquet. The third toast is traditionally to women (or to missing friends if you are a sailor). For this toast, men are required to stand up and drink to the bottom of the glass. "*Za zdorovje*" ("To your health") is the shortest and most popular Russian toast. The last toast, "*Na pososhok*," means "for the walking stick." It is the Russian equivalent of "one for the road," and is proposed to the departing guests at the end of a long night of celebrating. It comes from the times when pilgrims were invited to have a last drink before setting out with a staff on their long journey. Even the astronauts have the traditional "walking-stick drink" before a space flight.

Kitchen Talk

You will know that you are accepted as a close friend when you are invited to have a meal in the kitchen. This originates from the Soviet era, when people popped in to see a friend and the contents of the fridge were consumed, along with a bottle or two. Conversation was spontaneous and lively. During the Communist regime, when everybody was supposed to think and say the same in praise of the Party's achievements, opinions could be aired with sincerity in the kitchen: it was a more intimate atmosphere, and people believed that their kitchens were less likely to be bugged.

DON'T WRITE ABOUT IT!

Your Russian friends would be at best surprised, at worst suspicious, if they received a written "thank you" card. If they were to read about "wonderful company and delicious food," it would leave them wondering whether everything did indeed go well. A card is considered too formal, but the culinary effort of the hostess and the eloquence of the host certainly deserve a comment the next day.

Though one might find the Russian partying tradition excessive in food and alcohol consumption, and emotional display, it is an integral part of the culture, of bonding and socializing, and of friendships forged for life.

chapter five

THE RUSSIANS AT HOME

"I know now why Russians don't smile on the streets," commented an English tourist after her trip to Moscow. "Everybody is on a mission. They concentrate on what they have to do."

And although the bread lines are long gone the winter frosts still remain, and the proliferation of private cars creates traffic jams in the cities and problems on the highways (half of which are in need of repair)—so getting to work, taking the children to school, and doing the shopping are still a mission.

The Working Day

The typical working day starts at 9:00 a.m. and finishes at 6:00 p.m. It is common for private companies to hold early management meetings at 8.00 a.m. and to work overtime, but some businesses don't start until 10:00 a.m. So, if you are planning a meeting, find out the working hours of the company you are visiting.

Lunch is normally taken between 1:00 and 2:00 p.m., but some offices take it an hour later. At lunchtime the preferred food is hot soup. "Dry food causes stomach ulcers," your colleagues will inform you, every time they see you having a sandwich.

FAMILY LIFE

In Soviet times both husband and wife had to work to sustain the family budget; now a nonworking wife is often regarded as a status symbol, demonstrating that the family is able to live well on the husband's income. As domestic services come cheap, nannies and cleaners are in demand in the big cities. Many of them are former teachers or engineers, who find working for their wealthier compatriots more lucrative than working for the state.

Children are doted on, and are often overdressed and overfed. "Don't run—you'll sweat and catch a cold," is the most common phrase heard in the playground. Children receive a disciplined upbringing, with parents giving them little or no choice. They are brought up to be obedient, but are showered with love. You'll often see family scenes carried out in public, with mothers shouting at their children one minute and covering them with kisses the next.

Many young people continue to live with their parents after graduating from university, and sometimes the parents, if they can, support them financially well into their thirties. If in the West children are brought up to to face the reality of life on their own and become independent,

Russian children grow up knowing that their family will support and protect them in times of hardship. However, this family support comes with a price tag. The parents often feel the need to interfere in the lives of their grown-up children, even after they are married. And if they are unhappy with their son's or daughter's choice of a spouse, they consider it natural to show that. A very common story is, "They were very happy together, but the in-laws kept interfering, and now they are divorced."

Though living as three generations under one roof is less usual now, due to mass migration and the availability of rented accommodation, caring for the elderly within the family unit rather than in an old people's home is still the norm.

An Addition to the Family

"My dear," says Irina to her husband, "there will be three of us soon."

"I am so happy!" exclaims her husband, kissing her.

"I thought you would be," replies his wife. "My mother is moving in with us next month."

EVERYDAY LIFE
Family Meals
Breakfast can consist of a hot porridge— buckwheat *kasha* (especially for young children)

or semolina—omelette, sausage, or a cheese
sandwich. At lunchtime soup is a must, and if it
cannot be eaten in the office or at school, it is
served at home as a starter for dinner.

"Come, have something to eat," are the first
words of greeting for children coming home
from school, husbands returning from work, or
visiting grannies.

Everyday Shopping

It is no surprise that food shopping is a significant
part of the family budget. The food shops are
open from 8:00 or 9:00 a.m. in the morning until
8:00 p.m. Most of them don't even close on
Sunday. Some are closed for one-hour lunch
breaks. There are many private corner shops that
are open until 11:00 p.m., or even twenty-four
hours a day.

Gone are the
days of empty
Soviet food shops,
with long lines
and rows of canned
fish on display.
Russians have an
"as and when"

approach to shopping, buying dairy products,
bread, sausage, and ham several times a week. The
reason for this is not only the abundance of food
in the shops, but also that most Russian food
products have no preservatives, and as a result
milk turns sour and bread quickly becomes stale.

Apart from the universal milk and yogurt, some dairy products are distinctly Russian—like *prostokvahsha*, a version of soured milk, or *syrky*, small, chocolate-wrapped cottage cheese pieces, stuffed with jam or nuts.

The Russian answer to McDonalds is the sale of ready-prepared cooked food of many kinds; delicatessen departments well stocked with home-style salads, pickles, fried fish, baked meats, and *pelmeni* (the Russian version of ravioli) are very popular.

Modern supermarkets are opening on the outskirts of the big cities, and a Saturday supermarket trip is becoming increasingly popular. In Moscow, for example, you will find branches of international giants such as Britain's Tesco and the French Auchan.

Rynok, Yarmarka, and More

Russian food shopping is not complete without a visit to the *rynok* (food market). The food here is often more expensive than in the shops, and is considered to be fresher and of better quality. You can buy anything from vegetables and fruit to organic eggs and honey. The *rynok* is often surrounded by a *baraholka*, a clothes market, selling cheaper Turkish and Chinese copies of well-known brands.

The idea of the traditional Russian *yarmarka* (fair) has been revived. During the numerous religious celebrations rows of temporary stalls are set up in public places, selling fruit, cakes, sausages, and drinks.

Outside the exits of every metro or railway station there are food kiosks, many working twenty-four hours a day, offering such a wide range of snacks that you wonder how they all fit into such a tiny space. The government's attempts to eradicate them seem fruitless. Once removed, they mushroom again a hundred meters away.

You haven't experienced the Russian way of shopping to the full if you don't go underground. Literally. A well-developed metro network and a large number of pedestrian underpasses have led to the burgeoning of life underground. You go down the stairs and suddenly find yourself in a world of musicians, flower and newspaper stands, snack vendors, and video shops. One of the reasons, of course, is the weather—street vendors feel much happier there in winter.

HOMES AND HOUSING

As you approach any big Russian city, you will be driven through the *spalniye rayony*—the "dormitories," apartment complexes nine to twelve stories high. Built as state-owned apartments with municipally controlled central heating systems shared between one or several blocks, they are now being privatized. Not many can afford those apartments though—Moscow property prices, for example, are among the world's highest. Russians when describing an apartment give the number of rooms, rather than bedrooms. Most apartments have two to four rooms.

Urban Living

An American described his New York apartment to a Russian friend.

" I have a sitting room, a bedroom, a study, and the children's room. What about your flat, Vassily?"

The Russian, who owned a single-room apartment, replied, "My apartment's layout is very similar. Without the internal walls, however."

Most Russians can escape from those apartments to their *dachas*. *Dacha*, translated as a "country house," is much more than that. It is an integral part of the Russian way of life.

The *Dacha*

The *dacha* features prominently in Russian literature, particularly in romantic nineteenth-century novels in which city dwellers spend hazy summers in white mansions with orchards, the ladies perambulating under lacy umbrellas, the men drinking tea and discussing politics. Later came the postrevolutionary common *dachas*, the perks invented by the system for the "equally poor." The state would allocate a piece of land to a factory or research center, and it was up to the managers to decide how to allocate the plots. As a result of this land distribution, many Russians could afford to own their *dachas* without effectively paying for them. The *dacha* was the place for weekend relaxation, getting back to one's peasant roots, and, indeed, exercising the only right to private ownership the Soviet system allowed. During *perestroika*, when many people lost their jobs and prices were rising daily, *dacha* vegetable plots enabled many to survive.

The *dacha* is something that unites all classes, despite the differences between shabby huts and three-story brick mansions: the national obsession with rose bushes and strawberries, frost-resistant seeds, and current pests can only be compared to the British love of gardening. As Yelena, a Russian *dacha*-owner, has put it, "the call of *dacha* is like nothing else. It is as Russian as  vodka, caviar, and bureaucracy. I am drawn to that place with its outside toilet, built some forty years ago. I shovel sand, unload trucks full of gravel, and I am dog tired and grumpy at the end of the day, cursing the lack of civilization—and feeling righteous and smug."

SPORTS

Russians prefer watching and talking about sports to participating, but men sometimes organize weekend sessions of football or volleyball to keep fit.

Playing billiards (both Russian and American) is considered a status pastime for businessmen. Russian billiards is played with one-color balls, and the corner nets are much smaller.

Another favorite weekend activity is playing cards. Practically everybody does it on the beach, and men often organize overnight poker sessions, frowned upon by their wives.

EDUCATION

Russia inherited the rigid Soviet system of education where the main principle was "collective development," and punishment was more frequent than praise. Sciences were the core subjects; in the humanities initiative and free thinking were not welcome. *Perestroika* in society led to the democratization of the whole educational system.

Preschool

Free child care, the proud achievement of the Soviet system, still exists, though around 8 percent of the nurseries and kindergartens are now private. The educational principles that were dictated by the Ministry of Education have been replaced by a variety of educational development programs: Montessori and Waldorf systems; the "Emotional growth program;" "The path to find myself" program; "Making friends;" and even the "Young leadership program." With early training systems such as these it is not surprising that the majority of Russian schoolchildren want to become managers.

"Overworked . . ."

"What's wrong?" a militiaman asks a little boy who is crying in the street.

"I don't remember my name," is the reply.

"What about your parents' names?" asks the militiaman.

"No, I don't remember them either."

"Well, maybe you know your address?"

"Of course!" exclaims the boy. "It is: www.boy.ru!"

School

Schooling at a secondary comprehensive school begins at the age of six. School lasts eleven years, compared to twelve in Europe and the USA. This has created a serious problem, overburdening children of school age. Children aged six to nine have ten to twelve hours of schooling (including homework) a day; older children, up to sixteen. The situation is so critical that in 2008 the government is planning to introduce new regulatory standards to reduce the amount of schoolwork. Without a centralized educational program, every school, lyceum, or private gymnasium (about 10 percent of all schools are private) chooses its own courses, from the mandatory second foreign language to beekeeping.

The other side of the coin is truancy: around two million Russian children don't attend school at all.

Higher Education

The reform of higher education proposed by the government causes heated debates. Traditionally, the degree course in Russian universities lasts five years, with the possibility of a two-year postgraduate course and a further doctorate. The reform proposes the three-year bachelor's degree, with a two-year master's program to follow. Many university professors fear that this system would lead to superficial knowledge and ill-prepared professionals. The Soviet free university system is dying off: 89 percent of parents are willing to pay for their children's university education.

HEALTH CARE

Despite numerous attempts at health care reform, many health care practices remained unchanged from the Soviet era. Polyclinics serving a large geographical area remain the core of the primary care system, with separate clinics for children under sixteen.

The crisis in the health care system has continued for a number of years, despite the fact that Russia has the largest number of hospitals and doctors and the longest hospital stays in the world. Or, maybe, this is one of the reasons—with state subsidies diminishing, Russia's huge health care system lacks funds for new equipment and research.

MILITARY CONSCRIPTION

Traditionally in Russia the army was an honorable profession. There were military dynasties of officer families. The situation has always been different for soldiers, however. The Russian army is based upon conscription, and the eighteen-year-old conscripts serve for two years. There are plans to reduce the term of service to one year in 2008, and to increase the professional element in the armed forces. Professional military units operate in the Special Forces and in combat zones. As the number of military professionals increases, the required term served by conscripts is expected to be reduced further.

Many mothers, however, dread the *povestka*, the document confirming their son's conscription, much as they would a court sentence. They fear *dedovshyna*, the bullying and beating of recruits by senior conscripts, sometimes resulting in the death or suicide of the young soldiers. Another cause of apprehension is the threat of internal terrorism and the situation in Chechnya.

chapter six

TIME OUT

Russians love to stay at home (the Russian IKEA stores quote sofas and slippers as their best sellers), but there is plenty to do if you decide to go out. Museums and theaters, sights and clubs, concerts and hikes—the choice is enormous. "Cultural hunger" is a Russian expression: sometimes the lines for an exhibition of paintings or a new drama production are longer than the London lines for the Harrods sale. You can find entertainments to match not just your interests, but also your purse. In the capital, however, even the "cheap" restaurants can be quite pricey.

EATING OUT

Russian restaurants are far removed from the old, bland establishments with unchanging menus and cold soups. Many restaurants were set up as first attempts at private enterprise after *perestroika*, and the quantity is gradually turning into quality. You can find anything, from sushi to *shwarma*.

If sampling Russian extravagance is the goal and money no object, try the Moscow "Turandot" restaurant for lavish decor and an atmosphere of surreal decadence. Chinese food is brought on porcelain dishes by waitresses like dolls, floating around in eighteenth-century-style dresses.

If your wallet is slimmer, you can eat quite well in the mid-range Yolki-Palki chain, with *zakuski* from the all-you-can-eat buffet; or try the delights of Uzbek cuisine and relax with a *kalian* (hookah) in one of the Chaihana chain.

The Russian diet has traditionally been dictated by the climate, with mushrooms and berries in summer, and pickled or preserved vegetables in winter; hot soups at lunchtime, and slow-releasing carbohydrates—porridge, buckwheat, rye bread—to give energy.

So, what would you eat in a typical Russian restaurant, apart from the most obvious caviar and blini? You can try all sorts of pickles, which offset the sharpness of vodka, and *pelmeni* (meat dumplings), traditionally made in vast quantities in Siberia and then frozen (naturally, outside!) and kept through the winter. Of course, there is Russian salad, which in Russia is known as *salade Olivier*, after the French chef who created it at the Hermitage restaurant in Moscow in the 1860s. Be careful if you want a vinaigrette dressing—you might end up with a popular salad called *vinegret*, a vegetarian's dream, which is a mixture of boiled beetroot, carrots, onions, peas, gherkins, and potatoes. *Pirozhki*, pies with all sorts of fillings, are a popular street snack. Dishes inherited from other Soviet republics are also popular, and include Georgian grilled *shashlyk*, Ukrainian *borshch* (beetroot soup), and Uzbek *plov* (rice with lamb, slow-cooked with onions and spices).

TIPPING

Tipping is a matter for personal discretion. "New Russians" tend to be lavish. As a foreigner, you can round up a restaurant bill if you have had good service. In taxis, round up the fare.

If you think that vodka is the only famous Russian drink, think again—there are many interesting softer alternatives, such as *kvass* (a fermented drink made with rye bread), *kisel* (made with berries, sugar, and corn starch), cranberry *mors*, fruit compote, and more.

Venue with a Menu

When the Russian writer Joseph Brodsky was helping his friend Roman Kaplan with the opening of his Russian Samovar restaurant in New York, he came up with a collection of "gastro-rhymes": "Pelmeni for many," "Vinegret—you won't regret," "Beef Stroganoff if you're strong enough," "You won't be erring with Russian herring." The restaurant's popularity soared, and you can still order the same dishes there today, two decades later.

NIGHTLIFE

If after all this eating and drinking, you would prefer a more energetic night out, Russian nightlife offers plenty of opportunities. The English actor Simon Callow described the neon lights of Russian nightlife as "Las Vegas with Cyrillic script."

It seems that the years of grayness have made Russians desperate for forbidden fruit, well watered by the amount of cash flowing in the capital city (85 percent of all Russian cash is circulating in Moscow, according to unofficial sources).

The choice is enormous: from vodka bars and cocktail lounges to strip clubs, themed discos, and clubs such as Propaganda, promoting very different values from the ones on the red and white Soviet posters.

The casinos will soon bid farewell to the major Russian cities: in an unprecedented attempt to control the gambling business, the president has approved a new anti-gambling law, according to which gambling in Russia will be restricted to four zones from July 1, 2009, with super-casinos built in the middle of nowhere. Elsewhere in the country, gambling will become illegal.

ART

"We Russians need to feed our souls," commented an art collector recently. Sales at international Russian art auctions attract record bids, mostly coming from private Russian collectors, and occasionally from Russian museums.

If you are interested in Dutch paintings, the Hermitage in St. Petersburg has the world's largest collection, together with treasures of Russian art, silver, and Impressionist paintings. It would take you, the guidebooks claim, three years of daily visiting to see everything.

The Tretyakov Gallery and the Pushkin Museum in Moscow offer unique collections of Russian art. Wander through the Kremlin Museum, which recently celebrated its bicentenary, if you prefer to see the country's history through gold artifacts and armor, state regalia, and manuscripts. Don't miss the Tsar Bell and the Tsar Cannon at Ivan Square within the Kremlin walls. True to Russian tradition, they were cast to be the largest in the world—but were never used.

THEATER

Russian theater is thriving, exposing the Russian soul in both traditional and innovative ways. From MHAT, the Moscow Art Theater, to basement studios with several rows of seats, Russian theaters are eagerly attended. Note that there are usually several plays in a theater's repertoire at any one period, and the tickets for some of them have to be booked well in advance.

MUSIC

Russian music is a true reflection of the Russian soul: passionate, melancholic, and melodic, it embraces folk songs, Byzantine choral chanting, Eastern motifs, and Western harmony. There are plenty of places in Russia where one can hear this music, from church services to concert halls. Among the music festivals, the White Nights Festival in St. Petersburg is unique, as it is the only place that combines Russian opera, ballet, and classical music with the magic of the northern June, when night slips into day in one long, ethereal twilight.

THE CIRCUS

If you think you have outgrown circuses, think again. The circus has been the most popular and the most egalitarian Russian form of entertainment since the time of Catherine the Great. Skills are supported by four-year courses in the Russian State Circus School. Visit the Moscow Circus on the Tsvetnoy Boulevard, and your "inner child" will love the chimpanzees, admire the courage of those who enter the tigers' den, and laugh with the Russian clowns.

SUNDAY GUESTS

The most popular activity is still "getting together"—be it for a barbecue in the woods, visiting relatives for lunch, or, increasingly in recent years, at a café or restaurant. A Russian expression, *horosho sidim* (literally, "sitting pretty") means being comfortable with each other—people enjoying themselves together.

THE GREAT OUTDOORS

The Russian love of nature is not only reflected in the *dacha* phenomenon. It embraces many and various activities, such as day or weekend hiking trips, fishing, and mushroom and berry picking. All these activities, even though they may sound relaxing, are quite purposeful.

Hiking is often combined with some sort of celebration, such as school graduation, a birthday, or the beginning of a summer vacation. It involves a march to a particular spot (sometimes with a quick glance at the surrounding woods) for a picnic or an overnight stay in a tent. Mushroom and berry picking are often done out of necessity, rather than enjoyment. Having said that, it is the case that even rich Russians with *dachas* in the south of England are known to roam their private parks in Surrey in search of autumn mushrooms.

Fishing is the Russian equivalent of golf, or the most silent form of team building: it's the best form of escapism from and avoidance of the family chores. It is important to return home with a catch, though. The summer weekend markets do a brisk trade in fresh river fish of various sizes.

Hunting (shooting) is another, more upmarket,

team-building and trust-building exercise. Even if you have never held a shotgun in your life, don't reject the invitation—the picnic afterward might lead to one of your most profitable deals. Just follow the advice of the Russian politician Viktor Chernomyrdyn, who once said, "Hunting is my favorite leisure pastime. It gives me a chance to walk, to ramble, to wait, and to hide."

SPORTS

"Russians are good at sports," was a common perception even in the darkest days of Cold War propaganda. Russian figure skaters and athletes, hockey players and gymnasts are world renowned.

In recent years, however, Russian sports preferences have often depended on the hobbies of the political elite. Boris Yeltsin's interest in tennis led to the creation of the Moscow Tennis Cup tournament; Vladimir Putin's black belt spurred the opening of the numerous martial arts schools, and he has inspired an interest in horses.

The Russians love extremes, so it is not surprising that paragliding, parachute jumping, snow-biking, and water-biking are growing in popularity. And, despite common misperceptions in the West, wealthy Russians go to the Alps not just to spend vast sums of money on champagne and saunas, but actually to enjoy the skiing too.

For Russians, appearance matters, and it explains why gyms are not only popular, but also very expensive. A monthly membership in an elite Moscow gym can be around 1,000 US dollars. Do join if you want to see top international models (many of whom are Russian) getting into shape on a visit back home.

If you cannot afford riding or membership of an elite gym, then take your skates with you on a winter visit to Moscow. Skating rinks are everywhere, from courtyards in the "sleeping areas" on the outskirts of the city to the glamorous surroundings of Red Square. Visit Moscow's Gorky Park, and you will see the nation united, all ages skating together—and lining up together to rent the skates.

THE *BANYA*

The *banya*, or the Russian bath, is an institution. It is the epitome of Russian tradition, a club, and even a health center. Nestor, the eleventh-century Chronicler, described people running out of the wooden steam houses: "naked and joyous, they beat each other with birch twigs, and at the end pour ice-cold water on themselves, thus washing themselves, and not tormenting . . . ."

The procedure is quite simple: sweat for a while on the wooden bench, then somebody beats your body with birch branches to increase your circulation, then you plunge into the icy pool.

As a Russian Web site dedicated to *banya* has

put it, "The *banya* is not just for eliminating the toxins, increasing the circulation, and strengthening immunity. A person attending the Russian *banya* is permanently active: one needs to add some steam, release the steam, use the birch twigs, add some ventilation, judge the time to plunge into the icy water . . ." Therefore, concludes the article, "*banya* is a skill that requires not just knowledge, but also an effort from your soul . . ."

The *Banya* is a place for birthdays and business meetings, bachelorette parties, and stag nights. Traditionally female and male banyas have been separate. Consider the following advertisement for one of Moscow's *banyas*:

"We provide the freshest birch twigs and aromatic herbs. Our TV in the lounge has seventy channels; we have *kalian* and thirty brands of tea. Not to mention the karaoke set with fifty songs and three microphones . . ."

So if you are able to persuade yourself that birch twig flagellation is good for blood circulation, lowering cholesterol, and stress reduction, start with Sandunovskiye Bany, the most popular public baths in Moscow.

A word of warning, though: the *banya* acquired a negative connotation in the years after *perestroika*, and the term is often used for a seedy massage parlor. The *banya* has also become a tool of "black PR." Several politicians and businessmen have lost their jobs after being (sometimes only allegedly) filmed in *banyas*.

chapter seven

TRAVEL, HEALTH, & SECURITY

The great distances mean that almost everybody in Russia has been a long-distance traveler at some stage. The Russian road symbolizes new beginnings, returning home after long travels and hardships, and traveling through time, with new expectations. Numerous Russian songs and poems reflect these feelings.

Don't start feeling romantic yet, though. The famous phrase, allegedly Gogol's, that "Russia has two misfortunes: fools and roads," still holds for the roads. Not only are the majority in need of repair, but Russia also holds a grim leadership in Europe for the number of accidents and road deaths: over the last ten years, more than 350,000

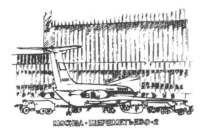

МОСКВА · ШЕРЕМЕТЬЕВО · 2

people have died in accidents on Russian roads. With Aeroflot increasing its Boeing fleet, flying around Russia is becoming less daunting. Beware of local airlines, though: a cheap ticket may mean a cheap form of transportation and a compromise on safety.

A TALE OF TWO CITIES

When you arrive in Russia, you will probably be landing in either Moscow or St. Petersburg. These two cities are the tourists' most obvious choice: not only are they the largest cities, but they also have the most theaters, museums, and restaurants. If you visit them both, you will also have a chance to see how strikingly different they are.

A Matter of Style

The following quotations from two articles about the attitude to skyscrapers graphically illustrate the difference between the two cities.

Moscow: "The construction of the tallest European skyscraper, 354 meters high [1,161 feet], will be completed in Moscow in January 2008. Nine more skyscrapers will follow. Living in skyscrapers is becoming increasingly popular among Muscovites. Moscow's mayor confirmed that skyscrapers are important for the city's prestige."

St. Petersburg: "The decision of the gas giant Gazprom to build a 390-meter[1,279-foot] tower that will ruin the horizontal skyline of St. Petersburg has caused massive protests from both experts and ordinary citizens alike."

Peter the Great's new capital of St. Petersburg was built as a classical European city on a grid, with long, grand avenues, canals, and bridges.

Moscow, the old capital, grew organically as a conglomerate of villages. It became the capital again in 1917. Moscow is a chaotic melting pot, dynamic and loudly wealthy. St. Petersburg is more reserved in a northern way.

Social and cultural differences between the two cities have been growing for more than three centuries. In April 2005 the Moscow-based company ABBYY Software House released an electronic dictionary of differences in the Russian spoken in Moscow and in St. Petersburg, which contained more than seventy entries.

DESTINATIONS

It would take more than a small book to list the places one could visit in Russia. For those on adrenalin-fueled quests, there is no shortage of options. You could climb Mount Elbruse in the Caucasus, which at 18,480 feet (5,633 meters) is the highest peak in Europe. You could trek around Lake Baikal, the "Blue Eye of Siberia," the deepest and oldest lake in the world; or bathe in the hot waters of the volcanic geyser streams on the Pacific island of Kamchatka.

For a real sense of adventure, to spot the elusive Siberian tiger, an International Red Book rare species, you can fly Aeroflot to the city of Ussurijsk in Southern Siberia, then you can catch the bus, then a helicopter . . . the Russian taiga stretches for thousands of miles, and is almost deserted.

If you prefer history and architecture, a trip around the Golden Ring of old Russian cities (Vladimir, Suzdal, Uglich, Yaroslavl) is a must. Remember though, in Russia distances are perceived differently, and if you are advised by somebody in Vladimir to visit the historic "nearby" town of Kostroma, it will take you six hours to drive there.

If the beach is your goal, try Sochi, a Caucasian resort and future Olympic capital. The hotels are astronomically expensive, so most people go there as *dikary* (literally, wild people or barbarians) and rent a room near the beach. If you don't want to spoil your vacation, though, try not to go home at the end of August, because the majority of the tourists will do the same, and you'll remember the two-day siege of the railway ticket office for longer than the golden beaches.

PUBLIC TRANSPORTATION
Trains

Trains are a convenient and reliable means of long-distance travel, although degrees of comfort and punctuality may vary from one route to another. There are several fast trains between Moscow and St. Petersburg, for example, with the Red Arrow traditionally being the most comfortable. You can book your ticket forty-five days in advance, but be ready to present your passport at the ticket counter.

Traveling by train can be your first taste of Russian communal living. There are three levels of comfort or class for long-distance travel. "Luxury sleepers" have two pullout beds. A "coupé" has four soft berths—if you are traveling alone you will be spending the night with three strangers unless you are rich enough to book the whole coupé for yourself. Last and definitely least, *platskarta* has six hard berths along an open corridor. Following numerous requests by female passengers, in 2007 the Russian railways introduced female-only and male-only compartments on its eight major routes.

There is a Russian saying that "the journey is halved with a good companion." Be prepared that a "good companion" in the Russian sense is someone who will talk to you and share his or her homemade food throughout the journey.

Brief Encounter

Recently a Russian national TV program, *Keep Waiting For Me*, which traces long-lost relatives and friends, received a request from a former passenger on the Trans-Siberian express. A woman asked the program to find a girl who had traveled to Moscow from Siberia in the same compartment with her and her son for the last four days of the journey. Apparently, these shared days had forged a friendship between the girl and the young man. Through the railway booking system the program researchers traced the girl, and the couple were reunited in the studio.

Local services around the major cities are provided by *elektrychky*, electric commuter trains with hard benches and no amenities. Avoid them on weekends, when everybody travels to their *dacha*, or on a "nature adventure."

The Metro

With traffic jams getting worse in the big cities, the underground railway network, the Metro, is undoubtedly the quickest and most reliable way to get around—if you can read Cyrillic, that is. All the lines are color coded, however. In Moscow, for example, the Circle line is brown. The Metro is open from 5:30 a.m. to 1:00 a.m. It gets overcrowded during the rush hours (8:00–9:00 a.m., and 5:00–7:00 p.m.). Tickets have the same price and validity for any distance.

If you have no time for museums in Moscow, at least try to visit a Metro station. Many stations are dressed in marble, with statues and chandeliers. Try Komsomolskaya station for the baronial, rather than the Komsomol, look; or Ploshchad Revolutsii for sculptures, or Kievskaya for images of cheerful Ukrainian farmers.

Buses, Trolley Cars, and Streetcars

Public transportation does not follow its schedules closely, and you might wait any length of time, from five to forty minutes. The public transport system works from 5:30 a.m. until 1:00 a.m. The bus stops are yellow plates marked with "A" signs, trolleybus stops are white plates with "T," and tram stops have "Tp." There are no buses, trolleys, or streetcars through the night. If you're late, you can only take a taxi.

Taxis

Taxi firms work around the clock, and you can order a cab by phone. The dispatcher will tell you the model and number of the car that is picking you up. There are also a number of official taxi stops around the big cities.

In Russia, hitchhiking (and paying for it) is common practice. It is cheaper to hail a car than take a taxi, but you should agree on the price in advance. The driver can turn you down if your destination is not convenient for him. You should understand the risks of getting into a stranger's private car, and don't do this at night. It is, of course, much safer to use a radio taxi.

Marshrutka (Shuttle Buses)

A number of popular city bus routes are supplemented by shuttle buses, run by private companies. They are more reliable, run more often, and will stop anywhere on their route at a passenger's request, in addition to their regular stops. You can hitch a lift on the *marshrutka* if there is a vacant seat and you are not standing under a "No Stopping" sign. You pay the driver when you board and, as with all types of transportation except taxis, you pay the same amount no matter how far you want to travel.

DRIVING

Hiring a chauffeur-driven car is a better option than renting a self-drive car. The main advantage is that the driver will take care of fuel, parking, maintenance, and dealing with "GAI" (traffic police inspectors), who have gained notoriety by their unpredictable behavior and a propensity for taking bribes.

If you are really keen to test the potholes for yourself, there are several rules to follow. To rent a car you must be over eighteen years old (Avis) or over twenty-five (Hertz). You must show your passport, have had a valid driver's license for at least two years, and a credit card (Visa, American Express, Europay, or Diners Club).

Russians often say, "The good driver is not the one who knows the Driving Code, but the one who can predict the fools on the road." Russian drivers are often reckless and pushy.

The official speed limits are 37 mph (60 kmph) within the city limits (though the Moscow traffic is often almost at a standstill)

and you have to do around 56 mph (90 kmph) on the freeway to be on the safe side.

To avoid any problem with GAI, you should always carry your driver's license and car registration documents; the car must be equipped with a first-aid kit, a fire extinguisher, and an emergency stop sign.

When oncoming cars signal to you, it is a warning that there is a road inspection or speed control checkpoint ahead.

Desperate Measures

The road police in the city of Kemerovo decided to fight speeding by placing cardboard cutouts of police cars on the freeways. Within the first month there was a significant increase in the number of road accidents: on seeing a "police car," a driver would slow down suddenly and be rammed by the car behind.

ACCOMMODATION

The high prices of the hotels do not necessarily guarantee quality. There is a niche market of small, cozy hotels, and there are also those of the Soviet era that cannot be allocated any stars at all. The paucity of world-class hotels has created a large apartment rental market. Most property companies in Russia provide safe and reasonably priced apartments for rent.

HEALTH

The health-care sector in Russia is overstretched and underfunded.

Health care is a mixture of NHS-type doctor's offices and hospitals and expensive private insurance centers. In an emergency dial 03 for an ambulance. Russian doctors often demonstrate the Russian values of compassion, patience, and resilience even on the lowest salaries and with a lack of resources.

No Frills Medicine

An American banker ended up in a local hospital in rural Russia after falling ill on the second day of the visit. "You must have traveled in Southeast Asia," concluded the Russian doctor after a brief examination. "You have a rare bacterium in the gut. You should do something about your bronchitis as well; don't let it go untreated."

After taking generic painkillers, the banker flew to New York to have an expensive, major check-up, lasting a week. The results said, "You have a rare Southeast Asian bacterium in your gut, and chronic bronchitis."

What to Wear

The obvious necessity of warm clothing in winter and practical shoes is worth a mention, as there are few sadder sights than frozen foreigners battling the elements in thin coats. A conservative suit should be your attire for a business meeting. Try to look reasonably smart when going out, as Russians judge people by their appearance before getting to know them.

SAFETY TIPS

While traveling around Russia, one should follow some commonsense rules.

- When traveling by train, lock your luggage or, if you can afford it, book the compartment for yourself and lock yourself in for the night.
- Beware of pickpockets both on public transportation and on the streets, especially if someone appears to bump into you deliberately.
- It is a legal requirement to carry official identification with you at all times, but it is safer to carry photocopies of your passport and visa than the original documents. Keep a separate photocopy of your passport and credit cards. Keep them somewhere safe; and don't carry all your things around together in one wallet.
- Russia is not as accepting of dark-skinned foreigners as other European countries, so be aware of possible extra police checks.
- Don't hail a private car in the middle of the night.
- Don't use an ATM on a dark street. Use one in a hotel or inside a nightclub, even if the exchange rate is less favorable.
- As anywhere else, try not to walk home on your own late at night. Courtyards and staircases can

be badly lit, so even if nothing actually happens it can be a frightening experience.

- Russian girls are attractive, and flaunt their femininity. Watch out, though: there are occasional cases of drinks being spiked with drugs in the nightclubs. If a girl invites you to her apartment, think twice. There may be a couple of ill-intentioned youths waiting for you outside the nightclub, or in the "taxi" that she is hailing.
- If you are really concerned for your safety, there are a large number of protection and security firms in Russia, staffed with former military, militia, or KGB officers. They offer a wide range of services, from personal protection to guarding premises.

chapter eight

BUSINESS BRIEFING

THE BUSINESS ENVIRONMENT

To understand the present state of the Russian economy, brave the pre-Christmas Moscow frost and venture on to Red Square. As you cross the vast expanse of slippery paving stones you enter a bizarre model of modern Russia: the capitalist consumer paradise of the GUM department store on one side; the founder of the socialist economy lying in state in his mausoleum opposite; and the red walls of the Kremlin, symbol of centralized state power, looming over the square. The glamorous skating rink in the middle completes the picture. Now scan the scene carefully.

GUM, the Main Universal Store, is the shop window of the consumer boom in Russia. The country is already the twelfth-largest consumer goods market in the world, and growing at more than 15 percent per annum. Car ownership has increased eightfold since 1999; consumer credit is rising 50 percent per annum.

Let's move to Lenin's mausoleum. The founder of socialism would have been overjoyed to see the socialist attitude to work (employment regardless of effort) still prevailing in Russian society, causing major problems for the development of the market economy.

The Kremlin has been the symbol of centralized power since the fourteenth century. The word "Kremlin" is often used in a more generic way to refer to the main government decision makers.

The Russian government established the National Oil Stabilization Fund to cushion a possible future drop in world oil and gas prices. Central reserves were worth $235 billion at the end of 2006.  The government continues to tighten its control over those industries defined as "strategic": natural resources and energy. A joke in Russia before the forthcoming presidential elections of 2008 went: "May 2008. The CEO of Ruatomgasoilsteelcoalaluminiumgoldprom, V. Putin, has received the President of the Russian Federation at his request."

As for the skating rink, figures for Russia's economic growth show the economy blithely gliding ahead, oblivious to the cracks in the ice.

Winston Churchill once said that the Bolsheviks created troubles for themselves so that they could successfully overcome them later. It seems that the Russian economy is now doing just that— successfully overcoming difficulties created at the beginning of the economic reforms fifteen years ago.

However, steady economic growth of almost 7 percent for the last eight years, with the most optimistic future forecasts reaching 9 percent, still has not allowed Russia to reach the GDP level of 1990. Growth is driven more by rising oil and gas prices than by internal production.

Oil exports are up by 55 percent. World Bank experts warn against the overdependence of the Russian economy on oil and gas. There is concern about the lack of growth in machine building and other industries and the lack of investment in scientific research and development: if EU companies spend around 7 to 10 percent of their profits on research, Russian companies spend around 0.5 percent, while 55 percent of Russian companies don't spend a single ruble on it. This problem, combined with a lack of modern management practices and a diminishing number of people of employable age, could lead to Russia becoming a raw materials supplier to the developed countries in a decade.

Wages are rising, but there is a huge gap in profits and remuneration: while 15 percent of the population reaps 57 percent of the profits, more than 40 percent of the population still lives below the poverty level. "There is no point saving for a rainy day in Russia: most of the population has nothing to save, and the rainy day is already here," says Ruslan Grinberg, Director of the Institute of Economy of the Russian Academy of Science.

Unpredictability

Ot sumy i ot tyur'my ne zarekaysa: "Don't rule out a pauper's bag or prison," is a well-known Russian proverb. Most Russians who made their money at the beginning of the 1990s experienced the "pauper's bag" to varying degrees during the financial crisis of August 1998, when the crash of the ruble almost wiped out the emerging middle class. Many fortunes were lost overnight.

An American businessman, working in Russia for several years, described doing business there as "riding a Russian roller coaster: you don't know when the sales will go up and how low you might fall, but the thrill and the adrenalin of it are great!" Volatility, he said stoically, is an inevitable part of business life in Russia.

Bouncing Back

The story of Sergey Chernikov is an example of the ups and downs of Russian business life. Sergey launched his first career by making soap at night, cutting up huge bars with thin wire. He went into partnership with the owner of a plant, and put his first million into renovating the production line, but after six months his partner cut him out, and his money was lost. Three years later Sergey had banked his second million from importing tinned food, but lost it when the bank went bust. His only possession now was a white Mercedes, so he started again as a cab driver. Now, at forty-two, his billion-dollar assets include a chemical business, a construction company, and packaging manufacturing plants.

The proverb gained new currency recently when the economy experienced a number of high-profile scandals, involving major Russian oil companies and foreign investors.

However, Russia is no longer "capitalism's wildest frontier," as described by Matthew Brzezinski, a Canadian journalist stationed in Russia in the 1990s. Foreign investment is growing at a steady 11 percent, and industries such as construction, IT, and retail are booming.

CORRUPTION

This is one aspect of the Russian economy that has remained unchanged for centuries. "You are wrong to think that I rule Russia. It is ruled by four hundred top civil servants," said Tsar Nicholas I in the middle of the nineteenth century. "I really sympathize with my successor. He will have a tremendous problem of corruption on his hands," said Russian president Vladimir Putin in 2006.

The top echelon of civil servants has always been a strong, influential class in Russian society—whether at the time of Nicholas I or in the twenty-first century. The *Nomenklatura*, according to the research of Russian sociologists, now constitutes a significant figure: around 5 to 6 percent of the population. With the breakup of the Soviet Union, the Communist *Nomenklatura* was formally dissolved, but in fact, according to sociologist Tatyana Zaslavskaya, 40 percent of top civil service positions are still occupied by the same people, or their children or other relatives.

According to the data provided by INDEM, the Russian "Information Science for Democracy" foundation, Russian citizens pay at least 2.8 billion US dollars a year in bribes. As long as the salaries of civil servants and public officials remain low, bribery and corruption will be an integral part of life in Russia.

The Soft Option

Several years ago a leading manufacturer of soft drinks built a plant in St. Petersburg, but could not start production because of a "failure to comply with fire regulations," as stated in the municipal report. The plant was eventually inaugurated six months later, with a new fire station next to it. The construction of the fire station had been sponsored by a "voluntary contribution" from the soft-drink manufacturer.

THE LEGAL SYSTEM

Russian companies often find clear-cut Western rules of corporate governance and transparency frustrating and claustrophobic. In Russia, every rule can have an exception, every law can be treated in various ways. Abiding by the law is not in the Russian mentality. Centuries of enforced obedience have given rise to habitual "inner mutiny": don't contradict the authorities, don't riot, but do things "your own way." Ironically, this survival tactic was one of the factors that doomed the economic reforms of the nineties: the majority of the population learned the imposed new rules, and did things their own way.

The Russian attitude to law in general and the unclear regulations of the first post-Soviet years have led to the development of a business environment based on unwritten rules. According to Dr. Alena Ledeneva, "these informal practices are important because of their ability to compensate for defects in the formal order while simultaneously undermining it."

Not easily understood or accepted by Western businessmen, these unwritten rules are the cogs of the Russian economy.

BUSINESS CULTURE
Blat and *Compromat*
The ingrained Russian principle of mutual support, "I'll help you and you'll have to help me," received an unusual twist in the Soviet era. The Soviet system of rationing and supposedly fair distribution was widely complemented by *blat*, the gaining of privileged access to goods and services, traded through personal contacts, outside the conventional distribution channels.

After *perestroika*, market challenges and the absence of clear-cut business rules saw the transformation of those personal networks into informal ways of making business decisions.

"Changes in . . . the economy have resulted in the reorientation of the use of personal networks toward a new type of shortage—a shortage of money. . . . The informal practices are both an impediment and a resource for the Russian economy, the Russian Government and the Russian people," writes Dr. Alena Ledeneva.

In the absence of the strong rule of law a grimmer type of barter has emerged and developed particularly in recent years as an alternative to weak enforcement practices. *Compromat*—collecting and using compromising information about business competitors or political opponents—is a widely traded commodity in Russia. It is used for destroying opponents, blackmailing decision-making officials, establishing market position, punishing rogue traders and unruly politicians, or simply as a bargaining tool in the deal-making process.

Personal Relationships

The right connections make all the difference between business success and failure in Russia. Russian culture is often called "high context" culture: it is all about relationships and liking or trusting somebody first, then doing business with them. Compare the statements of two Russian businessmen: "We work for months to prepare the business case for the investment project: due diligence, costings, the lot. Then the chairman of our bank goes to the sauna with the chairman of the company we prepared the investment project for. They come out two hours later and our chairman decides we are not going ahead with the project, as he does not like the personality of our client. Months of hard work wasted. It is incredibly frustrating." (The head of investment at a Moscow bank)

"When I meet a CEO of another company, a future client, or a subcontractor, we rarely talk about the project we are going to do together. All the details of preliminary work are already done by our staff; we don't worry about that. We have tea or something stronger and talk for half an hour about a recent film, holiday, or our kids' education. We decide whether we like each other and whether we can trust each other. Then we come out of that meeting and instruct our staff whether to go ahead with the project or not." (The owner of a St. Petersburg construction company)

"The best way to fight red tape and protect yourself from bureaucratic attack is to befriend a local governor in the region where you operate," advises a Russian business weekly.

Work Ethic

Everybody in the Soviet Union was expected to work. Soviet history contains many examples of tireless work motivated by sheer enthusiasm. Thousands and thousands of idealistic young "builders of Communism" were prepared to live in tents in harsh conditions and work twelve-hour days: the development of arable lands in

Kazakhstan in the 1950s, and the construction of the BAM railway in Siberia in the 1970s are just two such examples.

Selflessness

At the beginning of the reforms of the Russian energy sector in 1999 many of the 14,000 employees of the largest energy company, RAO UES, worked for months on end without salaries: they knew that leaving their shifts at the power stations endangered the safety of the electricity grid and the lives of Russian citizens.

Yet many Russian historians and researchers have noted the unenterprising nature of the Russians; their ability to work in short bursts of intense activity with long periods of doing nothing in between; their negative attitude toward entrepreneurs and wealth, and the firm belief that somebody "out there," be it another hamlet, city, or country, lives better than they do.

Russia is now moving away from the Soviet work ethic, where an employee was seen as an element of the *brigada* (a working unit), toward finding ways to motivate individual employees.

According to V. Mishcheryakov, head of the department of personnel development at RAO UES, there are three types of work motivation in Russia today. The first, and most popular, is the desire to secure one's job and one's salary, often in exchange for votes during the election campaign in a particular region. Agriculture is a good example: farmers are prepared to exchange votes and sometimes even land for the possibility of a favorable farming regime.

The second type reflects the desire to be included in the new economic order at any cost, working extra hours without additional pay, or self-financing additional training.

The third, still the rarest, type is personal responsibility for the company's results—mainly the prerogative of the owners of enterprises that are thriving in the new market economy.

We would add a fourth work motivation, ingrained in the Soviet mentality and very much alive today—the fear of punishment. The principles of the Russian prison system, the largest in the world, have been transferred to the workplace. As the HR director of a large IT company in Moscow put it, "The fear of punishment disciplines and motivates our employees. The skill of HR is to find a punishment appropriate to mistakes made and to apply proportionate sanctions." According to Russian legislation, an employee can be fired after two written reprimands in a year. Some bosses dish out reprimands for a late lunch or the wrong haircut. While such a system may breed disciplined and obedient employees, it rules out creativity and initiative. An ex-employee of the same IT company said, "the constant fear of sanctions was counterproductive; I could not concentrate and had to leave."

A word of warning to Western managers who attempt to introduce matrix management, appraisals, or individual key performance indicators overnight: certain features of Russian management culture, listed below, could bring their efforts to a halt.

MANAGEMENT CULTURE
Hierarchy

The Communist Party hierarchy neither held the leaders to account nor consulted with the people. Orders from the top were for unquestioning execution. There is still much of this mentality in management culture today. This is reflected, for example, in the reporting processes. The old "command and control" structure still prevails, with a strict vertical hierarchy and a single decision maker at the top. Generally employees expect someone to tell them what to do.

Even managers of small private firms who have MBAs from the world's top management schools are reluctant to delegate responsibility and share the corporate goals with their team. A common attitude is, "As it's my signature on the document, it's my responsibility and my decision only."

Waiting for the Boss
An American businessman visiting the office of a private firm in Samara was surprised to see a five-strong office team having a leisurely tea session at ten o'clock in the morning. "We're all waiting for Igor, our boss," explained the secretary. "The accountant can't go to the bank without his signature, the sales team are awaiting his instructions for the day, and I can't do anything without his orders."

Decision Making

There is a very slow decision-making process in public-sector institutions and large corporations. The main reason is the need to appeal to higher authority and the fear of punishment if something goes wrong. In the twentieth century, during Stalin's purges, shifting responsibility could mean personal survival. For decades the Soviet system followed the principle that "Initiative is there to be punished." As a result, the older generation of managers, who have had firsthand experience of the Soviet economic machine, are often reluctant to take risks and make decisions. A "yes" from a sixty-year-old director is very different from a "yes" from a thirty-year-old one.

Decisions are made faster in private companies with a young, dynamic style of management. Impulse decision making also contributes to that. Often, when dealing with decision makers directly, you will be surprised how quickly the decisions are made.

WOMEN IN BUSINESS

According to Goskomstat, 36 million women are employed in the national economy, amounting to almost half of the overall labor force. However, at the beginning of the 1990s unemployment among the most active segment of women, between the ages of thirty and forty-nine, was an alarming 18 percent (Goskomstat 1994 data). This is not surprising, given that women were the first to be laid off when the planned economy collapsed.

The Soviet experience of working full time, caring for several generations of the family, and running a household came handy. Women used their "transferable skills" of creative budgeting, multitasking, resourcefulness, and perseverance to set up their own enterprises. As a result, in Russia as a whole, some 40 percent of 890,000 registered businesses now are owned by women, according to the Moscow-based Federation of Russian Business Owners. Almost half of those women business owners are supporting the whole family.

"I admire our Russian women: twisted by their fate, broken by the system, often divorced, raising children single-handedly, they are strong enough to emerge from their ordeals with beautiful creative energy," writes psychologist Julia Bolina.

There is a darker side to this

female entrepreneurial revolution, however. As women were often quicker, more flexible, and more adaptable to the new economic environment than men, the divorce rate shot up, and there are now more than seven million divorced women.

There is another reason why women choose to start their own business, rather than work for a company. "Women can only reach a certain level in Russia; the highest level of play is for men only. The place of a woman behind a man is reflected in Russian Orthodoxy, in the Russian family unit. A woman in business has to be more professional than her male colleague to become a leader. Her success is often underplayed as a chance achievement, her authority is perceived as an exception to the rule," says Russian politician Irina Hakamada.

Women in Russia hold fewer than 10 percent of top management positions and earn on average 37 percent less than men in the same jobs. Out of twenty-four billionaires in Moscow, according to the Russian edition of *Forbes*, all but one, the wife of the mayor, are men. And there isn't a feminine form of the word "oligarch" in Russian, either.

MEETINGS

"One greets [people] according to their clothes, and says farewell according to their mind," states a Russian proverb. For Russians, image is very important and first impressions count. Wear a dark, conservative suit. Your shoes, belt, watch, and tie will be scrutinized—make sure they are in order if you want to make a favorable impression. Don't take your jacket off during negotiations untless the host suggests it. By the way, the suggestion to take your jacket off is a good sign: it means that the official part is over and you are getting down to real, detailed work. It is also a host's invitation to move on to a less formal style.

It is a good idea to have one side of your business card printed in Russian. Include degrees and qualifications—Russians respect education and professionalism.

Russian hierarchy is reflected in their greetings as well. The subordinate greets his boss first; a visitor is the first to greet the staff of the company he is visiting; and you should be first to greet those already in the room if you have just entered it. However, wait for the hand to be offered for a handshake, and remember not to shake hands across the threshold—this could break the good mood of the meeting.

Timing

The saying "time is money" does not reflect Russian reality. Your body rhythm slows down the moment you get off the plane in Moscow and join the snail of a passport line. This is reflected in a relaxed attitude toward timekeeping.

Be prepared for a meeting to start late, or to be canceled at the last minute. Be ready for the waiting game, when a secretary will repeatedly ask you to call again "within an hour," or inform you for the third time that her boss will be back "any minute now." Russians always advise you to plan a meeting first thing in the morning—in case you need to wait all day. The constant traffic jams of the Russian capital offer yet another excuse for being late. The meetings themselves might last longer than you anticipated. Plan your time accordingly. It is considered rude to curtail a meeting and rush off to another one.

Presentations
"I demand that senators speak in their own words, not follow what is written on paper, so that the stupidity of each can be obvious," said Peter the Great at the beginning of the eighteenth century.

Nowadays, if you want to make a favorable impression on your Russian counterparts, don't read your presentation, speak slowly and clearly, and maintain eye contact. Don't be deterred by the lack of reaction. Often the first presentation is seen as a preliminary step, and the Russian side will reflect and may even check some of your figures before making a decision. "*Doveryay, no proveryay*," "Trust, but verify," is a common Russian saying.

"Try to look welcoming. Don't scare your visitors off with your solemn expression. If you

are a true professional, you will still manage
to save face," is the advice given to Russian
businessmen by the Delovoy Protocol agency.

A Pleasant Surprise

*A delegation from a British manufacturing company
flew to Moscow to make a presentation to a
potential Russian partner. They returned to London
distraught: the Russians had not asked a single
question, and had not even smiled at the jokes of the
British operations director. In fact, the only comment
on their presentation had been a cool "Thank you,
we'll contact you." Two weeks later, to the
amazement of the operations director, he received a
fax stating that the Russians had really liked the
presentation, and that their managing director would
fly to London to sign the contract immediately.*

PROMISES

Russians often forget to return calls or messages,
or simply don't deliver what they have promised.
As personal relationships are crucial in Russia,
this is often done so as not to upset the person
asking, rather than to say "no." So don't assume
anything, don't get upset, just persevere.

A Russian manager called his friend in London
with a request to meet him at Heathrow Airport.
When he arrived at the airport, he discovered that
there were two more people in the arrivals lounge

waiting for his Moscow colleague. "I thought I should ask three people, in case one or two of you forgot and didn't turn up," was the comment of the arriving Muscovite.

BUSINESS GIFTS

Gifts are an important part of Russian business culture. According to the figures of the Delovoy Protocol agency, a businessman needs to give around two hundred presents a year to his partners, colleagues, and subordinates. And this is excluding corporate souvenirs.

Men should give presents to female colleagues and subordinates during the International Ladies' Day celebration, to the boss and colleagues on their birthdays, to men on February 23 (Day of the Defender of the Motherland, traditionally an all-male celebration).

If the exchange of presents occurs in a business situation, one does not have to open the box right away. If it is a birthday gift at home, you are expected to unwrap it and express pleasure. In a business situation a box is preferable to wrapping paper, as the office security might want to check it and paper could be damaged.

Finally, when the meetings end and the presents are exchanged, however tiring the working day has been, don't refuse an invitation to dinner. Toasting at the dinner table is a trust-building exercise, so don't turn it down.

NEGOTIATIONS

Facing negotiators who use the word *nyet* (no) more than any other nation and regard smiling in a formal business situation as a loss of face does not need to be daunting if you follow some simple rules.

- Don't rush straight into business; it is considered rude. You will be asked about your travels, hotel, even jet lag. This small talk is an important "warm-up" ritual. It shows the hospitality of the receiving side and also allows your counterparts to assess you.

- Remember that the Russians also have the proverb "*Don't change horses in midstream*," and avoid making changes to your negotiating team if possible.

- Be prepared for a hierarchical approach to negotiations. Even if the Russian team consists of ten experts, they will rarely speak unless asked to do so by the leader of their team. Have a leader of appropriate seniority on your team and try to mirror this approach.

- Russian negotiators tend to agree on general principles first and look at the whole project before getting down to detail. The Western sequential approach, with its step-by-step focus on details, schedules, and deadlines, might be seen as irritating. Be careful when formulating your initial statement; it will be considered the backbone of your proposal.

- "Maximal initial demand with minimal concessions" is a tactic often chosen by Russian negotiators. At the beginning of the twentieth century the philosopher Nikolai Berdyayev wrote about the Russian inability to perceive the "golden mean." The Russian national character is all about extremes, not mutual concessions; even logical analysis is based on opposition, not comparison. Compromise is seen as a sign of weakness.

- Your counterparts will respect professional knowledge, experience, and firmness. Save any final price concession for the last meeting, even up to half an hour before you leave for the airport. Face-saving is important to the Russians, so choose your battles wisely. Decide which issues are really worth defending.

- "The Russians keep their own secrets alike from foe and friends," wrote Winston Churchill. Though the tendency of keeping everything away from your friends, partners, and neighbors is diminishing, your Russian counterparts will still appear secretive as often they don't know how much information they need to present. If you need extra details, ask for them.

- The Russian approach to communication can be emotional and direct, with a lot of "*nyet*" as a best-case scenario and raised voices or long tense silences as the worst. Persevere; don't give up after an initial rejection. Change the subject, take time out, and then return to the initial contested issue. Be aware that phrases such as

- "We are giving you a fair price," or "Our offer is more than generous," can be perceived by

Russians as patronizing and could cause another emotional outburst.

CONTRACTS

The Russian saying "The agreement [contract] costs more than money," should be taken at face value: the agreement will indeed cost you much more than you anticipate if you don't follow the procedures. You should never rely on verbal promises. Even in certain situations, where people have a long-term proven relationship, we would not recommend this route.

Keep contracts straightforward and, wherever possible, conforming to Russian legal standards. The more complex you make them, the easier it will be for someone to find a way to breach them. A contract should be produced and signed in both Russian and English. Compare them before you sign. Bring your company self-inking rubber stamp with you—it is required as the official confirmation of your signature.

Sometimes, at the preliminary stage of negotiations, you might be asked to sign a "Protocol of Intent." This is generally not enforceable by law and is, in fact, a summary of the points agreed upon at the meeting and an action plan for the future.

chapter nine

COMMUNICATING

Personal communication reveals yet another layer
of Russian contradictions: people don't smile at
strangers, but a smile reserved for friends is warm
and sincere; eye contact in the streets is avoided,
but in business and personal communication lack
of eye contact is considered rude, if not suspect.

UP CLOSE AND PERSONAL

Years of communal living have accustomed
people to keeping a close personal space during
conversations. You may find that Russians stand
uncomfortably close to you. If they know you
well, there will be a lot of shoulder patting and
even hugging. Women are used to walking arm in
arm. Don't take jostling on public transportation
or somebody cutting in line personally. This habit
stems from the Soviet era, when people had to
"storm" a bus or train to get to work or push
ahead in the line to buy winter fruit for a child.

A handshake is the most common greeting,
particularly in business, with kisses and hugs
reserved for close friends and relatives. As we have
seen, don't shake hands across a threshold.

FORMAL AND INFORMAL ADDRESS

There are two forms of address in Russian: the polite second person plural, "*Vy*," and the familiar second person singular, "*ty*." It is considered rude to use the "*ty*" form when you meet someone for the first time, unless they are very young. Always use the polite form of address until you are invited to switch to the familiar one— a sign that your friendship with the native speaker has reached a warmer, more intimate level.

The polite form, "*Vy*," is joined by the name and patronymic—the father's name plus a suffix, "*ovna*"/"*yevna*" for a female, and "*ovych*" for a male. For example, Irina Sergeyevna means "Irina, daughter of Sergey," and Igor Alexandrovych is "Igor, son of Alexander." To address people by their first name, especially in an official business situation, is considered rude.

Patronymics

A British student visiting Russia for a language course was questioned by an immigration officer at Sheremetyevo Airport. "What is your father's name?" asked the officer. "Matthew," answered the student." The officer looked puzzled. "But your passport says that your middle name is Francis." "Oh," replied the student, "that's different. It is a family name. My father had this name, and my grandfather, and . . ." "But you have just said that your father's name is "Matthew," interrupted the officer. They were still talking an hour later.

There is no direct equivalent in Russia of Mr., Mrs., or Miss. The previous convenient unisex Communist form of address, *Tovarishch* (Comrade), is now obsolete. The restored prerevolutionary forms of address, *Gospodin* (Mr.) and *Gospozha* (Mrs. or Miss), though sometimes used, particularly in business situations, are not yet commonly accepted.

There are amusing and inventive ways of addressing strangers in public places. Any woman of preretirement age, in a shop or on public transportation, would be called "*Devushka*" ("Girl"), while a man may be addressed as something like, "Man in gray hat" or "Man with brown briefcase."

LANGUAGE
Speaking English
According to recent statistics, half of Russia's top management can read and understand English, and a quarter can use English in business. English is taught as a second language in most schools. While this is encouraging, Russians speaking English are often perceived as abrupt and rude, with requests sounding like orders and only rare uses of "please" and "thank you." This is quite unintentional: the Russian manner of speech is direct, and what may appear rude to foreigners is purely the result of stringing English words together using the Russian language structure.

The vast majority of the older generation, who

were brought up behind the Iron Curtain, don't understand English.

Speaking Russian

Starting your day with a polite Russian greeting might involve you in a tongue twister, with its clusters of consonants: "*Zdrastvujte*" (Hello). It's much easier to replace it with a rolling "*Dobroje utro*" (Good morning) or "*Dobry den*" (Good afternoon). Don't let the language structure put you off. Try to learn the simplest greetings and everyday phrases; this will be appreciated.

"I can always tell an American or an Englishman, even if he's lived in Russia for a long time and his accent is not traceable," commented a Russian professor. "The Americans smile too much, unnecessarily, and the English start every Russian phrase with '*Izvinite*' ['I'm sorry']."

Don't be put off by the heated exchanges you'll hear when your Russian partners talk to each other. Russian discussions are fast and loud, and to the foreigner often sound like a quarrel. Also, the intonation drops at the end of a sentence, making it sound assertive, if not aggressive.

Mat (Slang)

How about this for a contradiction? The Russian language has more words than any other language in the world to express emotions, and the literature is expressive, full of metaphors and unusual constructions. Yet *mat*, the commonly used slang, can express most needs and ideas in a combination of about ten swearwords. It is not just swearing, however. *Mat* is used (mainly by males) in all strata of society: by intellectuals as rude humor, by top managers as a way of releasing stress, and by many youngsters, sadly, to convey the simplest meanings. "I use 'nonliterary' words a lot, I have to confess. Not to insult an individual, though—I would never do that. More as a link between sentences," said the mayor of Moscow, Yury Luzhkov, recently.

SERVICES
Telephone

"You know you have been in Russia long enough when you pick up the phone and shout, 'Allo, allo, allo,' without waiting for an answer," claims an Internet joke. Often the caller does not introduce himself or herself either. "Ask him to call me!" or "Is Irina there?" are classic examples of the Russian telephone style.

The Russian relationship with the telephone is—yes, you've guessed it—contradictory. Russian loquaciousness and the low price of city calls

mean that conversations can last for hours. On the other hand, the telephone is not trusted. It is often thought that the line is bugged and the conversation listened to (not always without grounds); hence a phone call can be stilted, with a lot left unsaid, so don't rely on this if you want to clinch a deal.

Russians don't like talking to an answering machine. "A machine doesn't replace a human voice," is a commonly stated opinion, so don't be disappointed to hear the tone of a missed call on your machine. "When there is no message, just a sigh and a click, I know it's my Russian friend," commented a university professor in America. Similarly, if you leave a message on somebody's machine, don't expect an immediate callback.

If you have Russian business partners, you will already have experienced the curse of the cell phone: negotiations and presentations are often interrupted by those all-important calls. And yet interrupting is considered rude.

A cell phone company war is raging, bringing good news to network users: there are many cheap deals and packages to be had when you use your cell phone inside Russia. Or, rather, inside the major Russian cities, for a mobile signal strength in rural areas comes in one of three categories—weak, hopeless, and nonexistent.

The Internet

While Internet use in Russia is small relative to population size, it has been growing rapidly. A new poll by the National Public Opinion Center has concluded that 25 percent of Russians now use the Internet. The Moscow and St. Petersburg virtual communities are the largest—it is much easier to chat to your friends online than to venture outside at minus twenty degrees Celsius.

THE MEDIA
TV and Radio

Russia has close to ninety officially registered television companies, 25,000 newspapers, some 1,500 radio programs, and 400 news agencies—more than half of them independent, the rest entitled to full or partial government financing.

Judging by opinion polls, 82 percent of the Russian public see television as their principal source of information, and prefer it to the press. Radio comes next with 24 percent. Mayak (Beam), a round-the-clock radio station, which broadcasts news every thirty minutes, is the most popular. Private radio stations—Europe Plus, Radio 101, M Radio, Moscow Echo, Radio Nadezhda (Hope), Nostalgie, and others also have huge audiences. They broadcast information, analysis of the most important events, and music. The new radio station, Auto-Radio, telling the audience about the Moscow traffic situation and about everything connected with cars, has rapidly gained in popularity.

The Press

While television entertainment and glossy magazines are flourishing and dominate the media market, serious media outlets and journalism have been under increasing pressure from the authorities since 2000.

The top-selling newspaper in Russia is *Komsomolskaya Pravda,* a nationwide daily founded by the Komsomol organization and now owned by Gazprom. Its daily circulation ranges 700,000 to 3.1 million.

The business daily *Vedomosti* is supported by the *Financial Times* and the *Wall Street Journal.* It provides detailed, objective coverage of important economic, political, financial and corporate events, and offers in-depth analysis and forecasts.

Kommersant ("The Businessman") is a commerce-oriented paper, first published in 1909 before being closed when the Bolsheviks came to power and introduced censorship in 1919.

Rossiyskaya Gazeta ("Russian Gazette") was founded by the government of the Russian Federation. Acts of state come into effect upon their publication in it. The paper also covers daily news, special reports and interviews of government officials, and expert commentaries on documents of state.

Moskovsky Komsomolets is a mass-market daily, published in Moscow and circulated in eighty-nine regions of the Russian Federation, which addresses social and political issues.

CONCLUSION

When traveling to Russia for the first time, you go with your own preconceptions, based on the TV news you have watched, the music you've heard, or the books you've read. We hope that *Culture Smart! Russia* will broaden your understanding and make you a more tolerant and appreciative traveler. Discovering the Russian soul is like opening a *matryoshka*, revealing the layers, working hard to get to the gem inside.

You will be able to see beyond Moscow *tusovka* (party) bling and the grayness of the dormitory suburbs, understand the lavish grandeur of  St. Petersburg summer palaces, and the focused faces of the passersby in the crowded streets. When you get to the smallest doll, hidden inside, you will discover the true Russia: strong-spirited, compassionate, and warm. And then you might write a letter home, similar to that sent by a Frenchman to his girlfriend in Paris, after having lived in Russia for a year: "My dear Nadine, please come and drag me out of here. Because if you don't, I will remain here forever. Russianness is contagious—it grows in you and makes you so attached to this country that you want to stay, and never leave."

Further Reading

Figes, Orlando. *Natasha's Dance: A Cultural History of Russia*. London: Allen Lane, Penguin Books, 2002.

Hoffman, David. *The Oligarchs: Wealth and Power in the New Russia*. New York: Public Affairs Press, 2002.

Hosking, Geoffrey. *Russia and the Russians: From Earliest Times to 2001*. London: Penguin Books, 2002.

Ledeneva, Alena V. *How Russia Really Works: The Informal Practices That Shaped Post-soviet Politics and Business*. Ithaca, New York, and London: Cornell University Press, 2006.

Lovell, Stephen. *Summerfolk: A History of the Dacha, 1710–2000*, Ithaca, New York, and London: Cornell University Press, 2003.

Nordbye, Masha. *Moscow, St. Petersburg and the Golden Ring*. Hong Kong: Odyssey Guides, 2007.

Reid, Anna. *The Shaman's Coat: A Native History of Siberia*. London: Orion, 2003.

Service, Robert. *A History of Modern Russia: From Nicholas II to Putin*. London: Penguin Books, 2003.

Russian. A Complete Course. New York: Living Language, 2005.

In-Flight Russian. New York: Living Language, 2001.

Index

Acknowledgments

I would like to thank all the people whose insights into life in Russia have made an invaluable contribution to this book: Anna Litvinova, Yelena Khorishko, the Smirnov family, Matthew McClachlan, and Elizabeth Teague. I am also grateful to the Business Protocol agency in Moscow and The Research Center of Yury Levada for providing useful and up to date information.